# Teaching Mathematics with Insight

To the Cockburns with love

# Teaching Mathematics with Insight:

## The identification, diagnosis and remediation of young children's mathematical errors

Anne D. Cockburn

with illustrations by Peter Kent

ROUTLEDGE / FALMER
Taylor & Francis Group

UK     RoutledgeFalmer, 11 New Fetter Lane, London EC4P 4EE
USA    RoutledgeFalmer, Taylor & Francis Inc., 325 Chestnut Street, 8th Floor,
Philadelphia PA 19106

First published in 1999 by The Falmer Press

Transferred to Digital Printing 2002

*RoutledgeFalmer is an imprint of the Taylor & Francis Group*

**A catalogue record for this book is available from the
British Library**

ISBN 0 7507 0803 4 paper


**Library of Congress Cataloging-in-Publication Data are
available on request**

Jacket design by Carla Turchini


Typeset in 10/14pt Melior and printed by
Graphicraft Limited, Hong Kong

Printed and bound in Great Britain by TJI Digital, Padstow, Cornwall

# Contents

# List of figures

# Introduction and acknowledgments

## Introduction

Teaching is one of those jobs which looks deceptively easy. Parents send their children to school for the first time and, within weeks, they are delighted — but not surprised — to find their offspring counting, reading and writing. Indeed if these expectations are not fulfilled fairly early on then questions are asked and explanations demanded. Added to which many parents keep a watchful eye over their child's education for his or her entire school career wanting to know precisely what progress is being made and why there are differences between the standards and content of their own schooling and that of their child.

Over the past decade — let alone twenty or thirty years — there have been technological advances which have dramatically altered the way we live and work. Nowadays, for example, computers (personal and otherwise) are extremely common in the workplace just as videos are in the home. Who is to say what changes there will be in the next decade when our primary children are settling in to their adulthood? One thing is clear, however, we as educators would be failing in our duty if we did not endeavour to appreciate the implications of such changes and act accordingly.

Karen Fuson (1992) points out, for example, that, with the widespread availability of pocket calculators and the increasing use of computers, we now have tools which can calculate far more rapidly and accurately than we can. That is not to say that we should cease mental arithmetic and traditional mathematics immediately! Rather, she suggests, we need to change our focus, recognising human strengths and weaknesses and those of the sophisticated machines of the twenty-first century. Thus, instead of spending laborious hours on long multiplication and division, we need to develop skills as problem posers and solvers. In order to do this effectively, we need to ensure that children develop a thorough understanding of mathematics and the power of its potential. It is important to emphasise at this point that I am *not* advocating that we abandon the teaching and learning of number bonds, tables and other key facts: they too form an important part of the foundation of early years mathematics. This book is about the fostering of mathematical insight by encouraging greater understanding of the teaching and learning of the subject within the classroom context and beyond.

Target problem solving.

Originally the idea for the book arose from a realisation that, although I tended to tell my primary student-teachers that some aspects of mathematics were more difficult to teach than others, none of the books they read made any distinction between, for example, the frustrations of teaching place value and the relative ease of teaching addition to ten. How many newly qualified teachers, I wondered, have questioned their professional competence as they have struggled with the seemingly endless task of teaching time or the complexities of subtraction. Was there a way to calm their insecurities and make them more effective teachers in the process ?

These thoughts, coupled with my interest in children's mathematical thinking and behaviour, only slightly preceded a consultation document for a National Curriculum in Mathematics Initial Teacher Training in England and Wales (DfEE, 1997). Included among the proposals was the suggestion that trainee primary teachers needed to learn to,

> ❢ . . . *recognise common pupil errors and misconceptions in math-ematics, and to understand how these arise, how they can be prevented, and how to remedy them* . . .     (DfEE, 1997, p. 36)

These are laudable aims but the knowledge and expertise required to implement them should not be underestimated.

Indeed, to fulfil these aspirations I would argue that teachers require a sound understanding of the mathematical concepts which they teach and an appreciation of how children think and learn particularly within the classroom setting. Without such background information and knowledge teachers may present their pupils with a very limited view of a concept which may well result in pupil errors both now and in the future. An incomplete understanding of the equals (=) sign, for example, can create major problems for some children when confronted with sums such as, '6 = 4 + ?' Generally such pupils generally associate '=' with an action on their part rather than considering it as a symbol representing equivalence i.e. that symbols on one side of it were numerically equivalent to symbols on the other (Behr, Erlwanger and Nichols, 1980).

In this book I will argue that there are several aspects to unravelling the complexities of a mathematical concept and the often associated pupil errors. Given patience and insight, however, the necessary skills are well within the capabilities of any intelligent primary teacher.

The first chapter will consider in general terms why people make mathematical errors. I will then focus on four common topics teachers and their pupils encounter in the early years of schooling:
- the teaching and learning of place value;
- subtraction;
- time; and
- shape.

In the case of the first two topics, key concepts for each will be described in turn, together with discussions on unravelling the complexities and a consideration of possible remedies. The discussions on time and shape will take on a rather broader focus to add variety but, more importantly, to demonstrate some of the more psychological problems related to mathematics education. The book concludes with chapters on classroom processes and thoughts on the practical implications of this work on classroom practice.

Although much of this book focuses on potential problems it is not in any way intended to be negative or to apportion blame. On the contrary, I have the highest regard for teachers and learners and this work reflects much of what I have learnt from them.

Before I launch into my proposals I think a few words of reassurance might be in order: I am a qualified primary teacher with over twenty years' experience of working in the early years of schooling as a teacher, researcher and supervisor. I am now a senior lecturer in primary mathematics education. In this capacity I focus on mathematics teaching and learning in the early years of schooling. Whenever I can, I read recent research and attend international conferences to gain further insight into mathematics education both here and abroad. And, probably most importantly, I observe and chat to children, teachers and students as much as possible. Throughout the book I will refer to both my own and others' research but, as it will be interspersed with conversations and children's work, I hope that, at no time will it become dry and tedious.

One final point which you may or may not find reassuring depending on your perspective. I am a psychologist rather than a mathematician. I know what it is to be thoroughly confused and to feel increasingly stupid and incompetent when faced with a page of inordinately difficult looking mathematical problems. One of my aims as a mathematics educator is to reduce those feelings in others. I hope I succeed in my endeavour.

## Acknowledgments

The idea for the book was mine but, thereafter, I needed the help and guidance of a whole host of people. In particular I would like to thank the Primary PGCE students whom I had the privilege of working with in 1995–96 and 1996–97. I am also indebted to the Teachers' Group who contributed to the lively discussions we had in the summer of 1997. To Donna Alexander, Angela Hook and Peter Kent my thanks for making the production of this book so straight-forward and professional. Thanks, too, to my husband, Richard, for providing me with delicious meals throughout. And, finally, it is never easy commenting on someone else's work in a constructive, and yet tactful, manner but my brother-in-law, Mark, my parents, David and my publisher, Anna Clarkson and her colleague, Jackie Day, did so with the utmost skill and diplomacy — to you all my grateful thanks.

*Anne D. Cockburn*
*December 1997*

## References

BEHR, M., ERLWANGER, S. and NICHOLS, E. (1980) 'How children view the equals sign', *Mathematics Teaching*, **92**, pp. 161–97.

DEPARTMENT FOR EDUCATION AND EMPLOYMENT (1997) *Teaching: High Status, High Standards*, London: Department for Education and Employment.

FUSON, K.C. (1992) 'Research on learning and teaching addition and subtraction of whole numbers', in LEINHARDT, G., PUTNAM, R. and HATTRUP, R.A. (eds) *Analysis of Arithmetic for Mathematics Teaching*, Hillsdale, N.J.: Lawrence Erlbaum.

# Chapter 1

# Making mathematical errors

There are many reasons why people make mathematical errors. Sometimes mistakes are made through the slip of a pen or a moment of inattention never to be made again. Other times errors occur as a result of a slight misunderstanding or a lack of knowledge which is shortly to be attained and other times mistakes are the result of more fundamental misconceptions which are often difficult to unearth and which can take years to rectify. Some of these errors can be predicted; others cannot. Some are useful (see below); others are not.

In this chapter we will explore some of the most common reasons for children making mathematical errors in school. The discussion will not be exhaustive but is intended more as an introduction to give an overview of the most likely roots of an error. For many, much of this chapter may be familiar but, hopefully, it will encourage you to reflect more on the particular source(s) of an error(s) than you might have done in the past.

Figure 1.1 summarises some of the commonest sources of mathematical errors. Each will be discussed in turn but it is important to recognise that the causes are not necessarily mutually exclusive nor, indeed, that one can necessarily predict — or, at a later date, unravel — precisely how the various factors interact.

Before I launch into my thoughts on the reasons for making errors I think it is important to stop and think:
- firstly of our successes — most of the time most of our pupils get most of their mathematics correct;
- secondly we need to remember that mathematical errors are not inherently 'bad'. On the contrary, as a mathematics teacher I would begin to worry if all of my pupils were getting everything right first time all of the time for it would suggest that I was not challenging them sufficiently. Of course it could mean that I was a brilliant teacher but even I would dispute that brilliant teachers should push their pupils to their limits and how do we know we have reached a child's limits unless errors are beginning to creep in?
- thirdly mathematical errors can prove an invaluable means of gaining insight into our pupils' mathematical thinking;
- and, finally, of course not all mathematics is about right and wrong answers...

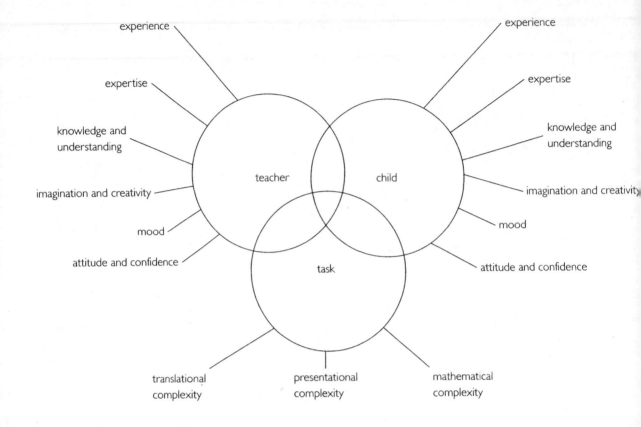

experience

expertise

knowledge and
understanding

imagination and creativity

mood

attitude and confidence

teacher

child

task

experience

expertise

knowledge and
understanding

imagination and creativity

mood

attitude and confidence

translational
complexity

presentational
complexity

mathematical
complexity

FIG 1.1
Some of the commonest sources of
mathematical errors

## Child: Experience

Without wishing to state the obvious: it would be a little
strange to assume that young children in a deprived area
of London had a detailed knowledge of everyday life in
provincial France (unless, I suspect, it was in a popular
television soap!) And yet, taking a less striking example, it is
surprising how many of us make assumptions about children's
experience of handling money and shopping. In the past, the
vast majority of primary pupils gained experience of shopping
by popping into the local corner shop and spending their
pocket money. Nowadays this is far less common due to
children's more restricted lives on safety grounds, and due to
the introduction of the plastic card. It is no longer wise to
assume, therefore, that 6- and 7-year-olds are experienced
money users: indeed, in the future, notes and coins may be a
thing of the past.

More generally mathematical errors and misconceptions
may occur when teachers make unwarranted assumptions

about their pupils' experience. In the case of money, lack of experience may be one of the reasons that young children who have been used to counting cubes, consider all coins — regardless of denomination — as equal in value.

## Child: Expertise

Although some may not like the concept, on entering school children have to learn to 'play the game'. I have written about this in some detail elsewhere (Cockburn, 1995) but, to take an example from Dickson, Brown and Gibson (1984, p. 331), Percy was shown a picture of twelve children with the following problem written beneath them:

 *'I have 24 lollies and I want each child to have the same number of lollies. How many lollies will I give each child?'*

*Percy's response was,*

*'I would give each child one lolly and keep 12 for myself.'*

Percy it seems, was 12-years-old but, despite his age, I would suggest that either he did not possess, or chose not to use, experience in 'playing the game'.

## Child: Mathematical knowledge and understanding

When a child makes a mathematical error the most obvious possibilities to consider are,

1 Does he or she know which procedure to apply? (e.g. does the child know that '+' means 'add' rather than 'subtract' or 'divide'?)
2 Does he or she know how to use the procedure correctly? (e.g. can the child do the necessary exchanging in the following sum requiring decomposition?

$$
\begin{array}{cc}
\text{T} & \text{U} \\
3 & 1 \\
- \quad 1 & 9 \\
\hline
\end{array}
$$

)

3  Does he/she understand the task both in terms of the language used and the mathematical implications?

Aspects of the above will be considered in more detail when I consider the translational complexity of tasks but here I wish to focus on language in particular.

Baroody (1993) considered, 'For children, mathematics is essentially a second or foreign language' (p. 2–99) sometimes, as teachers, we remember this but, I suspect, at other times we forget. For example words such as 'plus' and 'subtract' are obviously mathematical language but what about 'check' (more often a checked shirt than retry?), 'face' (what have people's faces got to do with plain, old squares ?) or 'take away' (a delicious meal?). Clemson and Clemson (1994) provide a useful list of 22 everyday words with specific, technical meanings when used in early years mathematics and I suspect, you would not find it hard to come up with a few of your own. Dickson et al. (1984) advise,

> ❝ The acquisition of language and concepts is a dynamic process. It is not an all-or-nothing passive type of learning. The child's understanding and use of language varies with the involvement of the child in the situation in which it is used, and with the relevance it holds for him. Since language development is dynamic in nature it is essential that the child and teacher should discuss various meanings and interpretations of words and phrases so each becomes aware of what the other means and understands by particular linguistic forms. The teacher is then in a position to help the child express himself more coherently. (p. 333)

## Child: Imagination and creativity

When you stop to think about it, it is almost contradictory that in the early years classroom we may strive for a really creative and imaginative piece of work in one session, such as English only to expect conformity and a decidedly unimaginative approach in the next. It may be a little hard to describe modern mathematics in such harsh terms as many teachers

Take the following. Desforges (1993) cites Jack Easley's (1983) example of Japanese children who were asked to describe how many apples would be left if they started with a bowl of three and took two out. The children were also asked to justify their decision. The first two children responded correctly in mathematical terms but the third said that the matter could not be considered: his mother had told him that he must never take two apples at once! All three children had been using their imagination but only the third had taken it beyond the realms of the classroom and into the real world.

E. It [finding answers] seems to be like a game.
B. (Emotionally) Yes! It's like a wild goose chase.
E. So you're chasing answers the teacher wants?
B. Ya, ya.
E. Which answers would you like to put down?
B. (Shouting) Any! As long as I knew it could be the right answer.

(Erlwanger, 1975, p. 10)

*do* encourage pupils to devise their own strategies to solve problems. Nonetheless, whether we like it or not, although mathematical *processes* are to be valued, mathematical *products* are often what it is all about: finding *the* right answer, by whatever means, is considered important. As busy teachers we may not always be tuned in to thinking about how a pupil's imagination or creativity might have contributed to a wrong answer mathematically but a perfectly logical response in everyday terms.

Most children quickly realise that finding *the* right answer is a major goal in mathematics sessions. Some do not find it easy as 12-year-old Benny illustrates, opposite.

Such frustration can result in children creating a logic based on earlier successes which can be used to explain their subsequent errors. For example, Erlwanger's Benny could add fractions — such as $\frac{3}{10} + \frac{4}{10} = \frac{7}{10}$ — and multiply decimals ($.7 \times .5 = .35$) but he made errors when, in effect, he confused the two. Thus, on being asked to add '.3' to '.4' he came up with '.07' explaining '. . . there's two points: at the front of the 4 and the front of the 3. So you have two numbers after the decimal.' (Erlwanger, 1975, p. 6).

## Child: Mood

As with everyone, mood can influence a child's performance. An individual's motivation to focus on the task at hand can easily be affected by whether his or her team won the previous night or whether he or she has just had an argument with a best friend. If you are not in the mood your performance may well not be a true reflection on your ability.

Similarly, carelessness — say if you are in a frantic rush to move on to the next activity — can lead to mistakes which might not otherwise have occurred had you been concentrating. Tiredness can also result in carelessness as I have discovered to my cost on occasion after an over-indulgent lunch!

## Child: Attitude and confidence

Children's attitudes to both their teachers and mathematics should not be underestimated when it comes to judging their ability. If a child has the potential to be a brilliant mathematician, for example, but is terrified of the teacher he or she may well find it hard to perform well. Similarly, if a child has been told that mathematics is extremely hard and only for the very able, he or she might find it difficult to fully participate for fear of failure. Such anxieties can result in pupils resorting to alternative, non-mathematical means — such as copying — to obtain correct solutions. This has been discussed in detail in Desforges and Cockburn (1987).

A child's confidence is not always easy to assess and to work with in an appropriate manner. In a study of first school teachers (Cockburn, 1986), I discovered that the maintenance of pupil confidence was high on their agenda:

> *If they [i.e. children] get hung up about anything when they are 5-years-old, what will they be like later?* (Mrs T, p. 215)

> *I like to find something they've said that's okay and build on that, because, if not, I think not very confident children get cut off and very put down. So you've got to keep the thinking process going. You have to kind of stoke it up and fuel it along all the time.* (Mrs S, p. 216)

Unfortunately, when teachers misjudge a pupil's level of confidence 'learned helplessness' can result. Mrs B., for example, considered mathematical confidence to be a high priority. She was quite clear that Thomas lacked confidence and when I observed the two of them working together (Cockburn, 1986) that certainly appeared to be the case: 5-year old Thomas worked very slowly and was constantly turning to Mrs B. looking for help and reassurance. When I assessed Thomas' mathematical abilities, however, it was more than clear that he was extremely quick and able. In this particular case I do not think Thomas' dependence on Mrs B. necessarily resulted in him making errors. The point I wish to make though is that misjudging levels of confidence can influence mathematical performance.

## Task: Mathematical complexity

If a task is too challenging for a child errors may well result. Ausubel (1986) once remarked,

> If I had to reduce all educational psychology to just one principle I would say this: the most important single factor influencing learning is what the child already knows. Ascertain this and teach him [her] accordingly. (p. iv)

This might seem to be stating the obvious but, as Bennett, Desforges, Cockburn and Wilkinson (1984) observed, matching mathematical tasks to pupils' levels of attainment is not as easy as one might imagine. If a child makes an error, therefore, I would suggest that checking the mathematical complexity of the task in relation to the child's knowledge is an obvious first step.

## Task: Presentational complexity

Another important point to check when an error occurs is to ensure that the task is presented in an appropriate manner. For example, worksheets are sometimes covered in writing which could be making it difficult for a child to know how to proceed. Aspects of this will be considered in more detail in the next section, but the point I wish to make here is that errors can occur if the presentation of a task is inappropriate and interferes with the child being able to tackle the mathematics.

## Task: Translational complexity

A third major source of mathematical error is a child's inability to translate a task in the manner intended. The five most common aspects of this are:

■ **translating the mathematics:** in other words, does the child know what is required of them in mathematical terms? This difficulty typically arises when children are faced with word problems. For example, a problem such as 'Sam and Jo share the cost of a bag of sweets. Sam paid 15p and Jo paid 30p. How much did the bag cost?' might well result in a pupil assuming division is required as the word 'share' is involved. I am not against such problems per se as I think they are an indication of a child's facility to decipher the fundamental requirements of a task — a most useful ability in everyday life.

Translation problems can also occur when a child has been working on a series of, say, addition sums and is suddenly faced with a subtraction sum. A frequent tendency is to add rather than subtract resulting in $6 - 4 = 10$.

- **reading errors:** recently, when I cited an example from Dickson et al. (1984) of 12-year-old Jane confusing 'angle' and 'angel' I was surprised to see quite so many embarrassed grins among my audience: clearly the problem was not confined to Jane! Sometimes such errors go undetected but, in this case, the confusion was uncovered when Jane asked,

> ❝ When it says here, 'Which angel is the right angel?' does it mean that the wings should go this way, or that way?
>
> (Dickson et al., 1984, p. 336)

Obviously reading errors are more likely to occur with young and inexperienced readers.

- **comprehension errors:** sometimes pupils have difficulty in understanding the written aspects of a problem. This is not necessarily the same as simply translating the mathematics as described above. Comprehension errors occur when a child does not yet have the ability to understand a word or a phrase. He or she may be able to read it — just as you can read 'discerp' — and yet not know what it means. (In case you are wondering, 'discerp' means 'to separate.') It is certainly a type of translation fault but I would argue that not all translation errors are comprehension errors for, in the case of the former, a child may well know the range of possible meanings of a word or phrase but have failed to use the appropriate translation for the situation. In the case of comprehension errors, however, a child does not understand the word(s) used.

■ **encoding errors** occur when children have no difficulty in completing the mathematics required of them but they sometimes fail to encode their responses in an appropriate manner, e.g. '6' rather than '6p'; '19' instead of '91' or '$^2/_4$' when '$^1/_2$' is expected.

■ **implication errors:** if a child does not appreciate the reality of a problem he or she can make an error. This can arise as the result of one of the above difficulties (e.g. a failure to comprehend) and an over-, or even under-, active imagination! For example, consider the following problem,

> *If each bus can take 24 people and 97 people wish to travel by bus, how many buses will be required? Some children might reply 'four' because they have been working on rounding up or down to the nearest five or because they can picture the ninety-seventh person sitting on the ninety-sixth's lap!*

## Teacher: Attitude and confidence

Just as a child's attitude and confidence can influence mathematical performance so too can a teacher's. Indeed, when studying primary teachers' stress, 69.9 per cent of the 335 respondents said that 'thorough lesson preparation' was a very effective way of coping with their stress. If, however, they lack confidence *and* dislike the subject they *may* find it difficult to work up the enthusiasm to teach mathematics in an effective manner thus increasing the likelihood of errors.

If we are honest, it is also true to say that some teachers do not like some pupils. It is also true to say that in some classroom relationships there is a phenomenon called 'the self-fulfilling prophecy' in operation. Good and Brophy (1987) explain that this term was first coined by Merton in 1948 and refers to, 'an originally erroneous expectation [which] leads to behaviour that causes the expectation to become true' (p. 116). This does not tend to be a problem if an average child is labelled bright and treated accordingly. Problems can arise, however, if an able child (such as Thomas discussed above) is labelled not very able or lacking in confidence. It may not be long before that child ceases to perform to the best of their ability.

When teachers lack confidence in their mathematical abilities they sometimes overcompensate and ensure that they prepare their lessons extremely thoroughly.

## Teacher: Mood

It takes little imagination to appreciate that when someone is pushed for time or feeling generally pressurised they do not perform to the best of their ability. Hurried explanation coupled, perhaps, with a less sensitive monitoring of pupil responses may well result in a higher number of mathematical errors than might typically occur. As professionals we try to minimise the impact of external demands on our classroom performance but, as humans, this is not always possible.

## Teacher: Imagination and creativity

Below I will discuss teachers' knowledge, expertise and experience all of which naturally develop and mature (one hopes!) as one's career proceeds. Imagination and creativity, however, are slightly different in so far as they require not only the ability to recognise when, for example, something has gone wrong, but also the wherewithal to reflect on the situation and to do something about it.

Take a situation where a teacher is trying to encourage her class to think of subtraction in broader terms than 'taking away'. She introduces the session with plenty of practical examples comparing the heights of various objects — 'How much taller is this pencil than that pencil?'; 'How much shorter is that book than that book' and so on. She then gives the children a series of well-illustrated examples to work through. All goes well until Sam is posed with the question 'What is the difference in height between Marizta and Ben?' There are clues as to what is required (i.e. pictures of Marizta and Ben with tape measures beside them and the word 'height' in the problem), but what catches Sam's eye is the word 'difference'. This triggers him into listing all the differences between Marizta and Ben: Marizta is a girl and Ben is a boy; Marizta is wearing beautiful clothes but Ben looks a bit scruffy; Marizta has black hair but Ben has blond, and so on. There is little doubt that teachers would pick up on the reasons for Sam's misunderstanding, appreciate that they had not signalled the word 'difference' as a mathematical term in their introduction and then proceed to explain what it means with reference to subtraction.

Often, however, such confusions are less easy to detect and rectify. One reason is that children, unlike Sam above, usually come up with numerical answers and so it is easy to assume that they have made a simple error in calculation rather than misinterpreted the question. Another reason is that some teachers have a marked tendency to repeat their instructions over again in exactly the same manner: it is no good repeating 'You need to add the two and the four to find out how much they make altogether' if a child has no idea what 'add' means, having only used the term 'and' in the past. An imaginative and creative teacher faced with such a situation may well think back to his or her instructions, try to imagine why the child might not be responding as anticipated and find a creative way of presenting the material in a manner the child understands.

## Teacher: Knowledge

Perhaps, surprisingly, a teacher with too little *or* too much mathematical knowledge can increase the likelihood of pupil errors. If a teacher's mathematical knowledge is limited he or she may not appreciate the wide variety of guises in which subtraction may appear (see Chapter 4). Thus, quite unwittingly, he or she may be laying down problems for children in later life. For example, if pupils are only taught to associate the minus sign ('−') with taking away the smaller number from the bigger, then it is not surprising that they present answers such as '$6 - (-7) = 1$' further up the school.

This year my initial teacher training students also reported that some of them had made errors at school because their teachers knew too much mathematics! Basically they described how their teachers had quickly explained something to them in great detail, they had not understood and had asked for help. They were then given another hasty explanation but had still failed to grasp what was required of them. Rather than risk appearing stupid they had then resorted to non-mathematical means of completing their mathematics. Such strategies (e.g. copying, overhearing someone else's response and looking up the answer) are discussed in more detail in Chapter 10.

## Teacher: Expertise

As I said earlier in the chapter, the categories discussed here are not mutually exclusive and there is certainly overlap between this and the other teacher attributes described. Although it involves aspects of the other skills considered, however, I think it is important to consider the role of teacher expertise in its own right. I am not referring here specifically to mathematical expertise but rather to the broader expertise of a skilled educator. It is the ability to communicate with children in such a way that you make them feel comfortable and can instigate a real dialogue about, among other things, their knowledge, skills and understanding.

Certainly language often plays an important part in the communication process but there are other more subtle, but equally important, factors at work. These include the way teachers position themselves (e.g. a towering teacher conveys a rather different message to one sitting at the same level as a child), the tone of voice (e.g. quiet and calm or loud and inquisitorial?) and the perceived attention given (e.g. does the child feel that he or she has the teacher's concentration or is he or she one of several snatching a brief word at the teacher's desk). Such expertise can be difficult to cultivate and display in a busy classroom environment, but without it I would suggest that some pupils feel neglected and their mathematics suffers accordingly.

## Teacher: Experience

Education is one of those subjects on which everyone has an opinion: we — or at least the vast majority of us — have been to school and so we must know what we are talking about! Sometimes this can be very irritating but, more importantly, I think it denies the wealth of experience that teachers acquire over the years. As a teacher educator I have observed that not all teachers can articulate how and why they operate in the way they do but it is clear from watching many of them that they know exactly how to provide effective learning environments and how to respond when the unexpected occurs.

In terms of mathematics education the most successful teachers not only acquire a fund of information about children's errors over the years but they also become increasingly aware of the range of behaviours that pupils engage in to avoid doing any mathematics at all! This book is about taking such experience a stage further by encouraging teachers to reflect on this valuable information, using it to predict possible mathematical errors and hence minimising their *unwarranted* occurrence in the future for, as I said at the beginning of this chapter, not all errors are necessarily to be avoided.

## References

Ausubel, D.P. (1968) *Educational Psychology: A Cognitive View*, New York: Holt, Rinehart and Winston.

Baroody, A.J. (1993) *Problem Solving, Reasoning and Communicating*, New York: Macmillan.

Bennett, N., Desforges, C., Cockburn, A. and Wilkinson, B. (1984) *The Quality of Pupil Learning Experiences*, London: Lawrence Erlbaum Associates.

Clemson, D. and Clemson, W. (1994) *Mathematics in the Early Years*, London: Routledge.

Cockburn, A.D. (1986) 'An empirical study of classroom processes in infant mathematics education', unpublished PhD thesis, University of East Anglia.

Cockburn, A.D. (1995) 'Learning in classrooms', in Desforges, C. (ed.) *An Introduction to Teaching: Psychological Perspectives*, Oxford: Blackwell.

Cockburn, A.D. (1996) *Teaching Under Pressure*, London: Falmer Press.

Desforges, C. (1993) *Children as Thinkers and Learners,* London: British Association of Early Childhood Education.

Desforges, C. and Cockburn, A. (1987) *Understanding the Mathematics Teacher*, London: Falmer Press.

Dickson, L., Brown, M. and Gibson, O. (1984) *Children Learning Mathematics*, London: Cassell.

ERLWANGER, S. (1975) *The Observation–Interview Method and Some Case Studies*, mimeo: University of Illinois.

GOOD, T. and BROPHY, J. (1987) *Looking in Classrooms*, New York: Harper and Row.

## Chapter 2    Starting with place value

In the last chapter I discussed general reasons why children might make mathematical errors. Here I become more specific: by focusing on the general and the specific I think we can broaden our understanding of mathematics education to good effect. Before teaching any topic, let alone considering the potential problems which might be associated with it, I think it is important to establish as clear a mathematical understanding of the topic as possible. In this chapter, therefore, I will briefly outline the basic principles of place value with the necessary prerequisite skills children require to tackle it. In the next chapter we will explore some of the difficulties associated with the teaching and learning of the fundamental concepts involved. Should your mathematics be sound you might well wish to skip to Chapter 3 where the basic message of the book really begins.

## The basic concept

There are four basic features when it comes to appreciating the meaning of place value.

- The first is that in the Hindu–Arabic system we use for counting there are ten basic symbols: 0, 1, 2, 3, 4, 5, 6, 7, 8 and 9. Each of these are called *digits*.

- The second point is that the position of a digit relative to any other digits determines its value. Thus the sixes in the following *numerals* (i.e. the marks on the paper between the inverted commas) all have a different value: '6', '65', '654', '6543', '65432', '654321' and '6543210'. Hence the term *place value*.

- The third feature is that every time a digit is 'moved' one position further to the left (as above) it has, in effect, been multiplied by ten. Thus the six in '65' represents ten times more than the six in '6'; the six in '654' is worth ten times ten more and so on. To determine the value of any digit within a numeral therefore it is necessary to take into account its value and how many digits there are to the right of it. In the numeral '6543' the digit six is worth its value of 6 multiplied by $10 \times 10 \times 10$ as there are three digits to the right of it i.e. 6000.

- The final important factor regarding place value is that, to quantify the size of a numeral, you need to evaluate each of the digits within it, add them together and hence arrive at a composite value. Thus '65432' is made up of:
  - a six digit worth $6 \times 10 \times 10 \times 10 \times 10$, in other words sixty thousand
  - a five digit worth $5 \times 10 \times 10 \times 10$, in other words five thousand
  - a four digit worth $4 \times 10 \times 10$, in other words four hundred
  - a three digit worth $3 \times 10$, in other words thirty and
  - a two digit
  - making a total of sixty-five thousand, four hundred and thirty-two.

Determining the value of 6543210 is a harder proposition because we have a tendency to read from left to right. The majority of us, however, find this difficult to do when faced with long numbers and most of us resort to working from right to left in the first instance. Thus with 6543210 my tendency would be to group the digits into threes: 6543210 becomes 6543 210 and then 6 543 210 making the six digit worth six million, the five digit worth five hundred thousand and so on until you end up with six million, five hundred and forty-three thousand, two hundred and ten.

Described like that, to my mind, place value sounds quite simple and straight-forward. A little laborious perhaps when you come to large numbers but, nonetheless, not very difficult. Added to which young children are not generally confronted by such vast numbers at the outset of their school career so why is the teaching and learning of it apparently so difficult? The answer will be explored in detail in the next chapter but, first, it may be enlightening to consider some of the prerequisite skills required to even begin to have an appreciation of place value.

## Prerequisite skills

### Counting

Before children move on to the dizzy heights of tens and units they need to have acquired a sound understanding of digits, i.e. the numbers '0' to '9'. As adults it is probably difficult for us to recall the complexities of learning to count. Indeed, I suspect most of us had few, if any, problems. As we learnt our numbers we gradually acquired some basic — but critical — concepts. We may not have been particularly aware of them but, without their acquisition, we certainly would have been unable to be where we are today.

One of the earliest mathematical skills a child develops is the ability to recite numbers. Initially the words may not be in the correct order (e.g. '1, 2, 6, 7') and, indeed, there may be some repetition (e.g. '1, 2, 6, 7, 1, 3, 2'). Gradually children develop the correct 'stable order principle' (Gelman and Gallistell, 1978) which means that they can recite the correct numbers in the correct order consistently. Although this is a real achievement, however, it does not necessarily mean that the children can count effectively.

Imagine a young child, Jim, with six sweets in front of him (Figure 2.1). To count them it is likely that he will have to

IG 2.1
m demonstrating the principles
f counting

point to each in turn assigning a number name as he does so. This is often called 'tagging'. To tag effectively Jim needs to keep a check on which sweets he has counted and which are still left to be counted. Thus, having counted the two lefthand sweets in Figure 2.1, he needs to recognise that he has no need to count them again but that his remaining task is to count the sweets to the right of them. This is fairly easy if Jim is not distracted and the sweets are in a straight line as shown. It is considerably harder if they are in a circle or in a bundle: Which sweet did he start with? Which are still to be counted?

Jim also needs to be aware of the fact that counting involves *temporarily* assigning one number name to each object as he points to it and that the last number he says — in this case 'six' — has special significance. Not only is it the number given to the righthand sweet but that it also represents the total number of items in the group.

Gelman and Gallistell (1978) describe two further principles which are an implicit part of our counting skills. The first is the 'order irrelevance principle'. Jim chose to count the sweets in Figure 2.1 from left to right but he might equally well have opted to count them from right to left or even started in the middle. In other words, the sequence in which you count objects is irrelevant: it makes no difference whatever to the total number of items to be counted. People sometimes wonder why it is necessary to articulate such a principle. One important reason in the early years is that children are learning vast amounts and that — to some — there could appear to be all manner of inconsistencies in what they are taught. For example, as discussed, Figure 2.1 represents six sweets irrespective of the way in which they are counted but, turning to another learning situation, 'w-a-s' is not at all the same as 's-a-w' or even 'a-s-w' or 'a-w-s'. It is incredible that children learn that order is crucial in some situations but not in others when so few teachers tell them that this is the case.

The second principle Gelman and Gallistell (1978) describe is the 'abstraction principle'. This is extremely useful as it allows you to count objects you cannot see at the time of counting. For example, how many rooms do you have in your house? As an experienced counter you may need to 'picture' the rooms, but I would be most surprised — unless you lived in a very big mansion — that you would have to go and point at them as you counted. Having acquired the abstraction principle you can also count totally imaginary objects: indeed you can count anything you like!

## Reading and writing numbers

Although a child might be able to count effectively well into the teens and beyond, it is important that they can write the numbers '0' to '9' in a conventional manner before they proceed to formal work on place value. They need to be secure in the knowledge that '7' represents seven items and that it is always written '7' rather than 'Γ'.

(Having said that I am *not* in favour of rushing them in to laborious sessions on how to write numbers correctly. I much prefer Hughes' (1986) view that such work should not be rushed and that it is perfectly acceptable for young children to represent quantities in ways that they see fit until they have a sound understanding of the underlying concepts of number and are naturally ready to proceed to more orthodox methods of recording.)

## Manipulating numbers

Prior to investigating the intricacies of place value, children need to be secure in their ability to work with the numbers '0' to '9'. They need to gain a sense of what the numbers mean and how they relate to one another: that 'five add one is six' is another way of saying 'three add three' or 'nine subtract three' or even, 'two times three' and so on. Without such confidence, the array of increasingly large numbers before them will appear very sterile and have little, or no, real significance for them. They need to appreciate, for example, that the numerical difference between four and five is the same as between eight and nine for, without that, how can they begin to understand that the difference between forty and fifty is the same as between eighty and ninety?

## Zero

Finally, a special mention of zero. There are ten digits and, as I have done above, I tend to record them as '0' to '9'. In

**Suggestion**

**Task 1:** The '6' in 654 is worth how many times more than the value of the '6' in 65432: 100, 10, $\frac{1}{10}$ or $\frac{1}{100}$?

**Task 2:** The '6' in 65432 is how many times greater in value than the '3': 20, 100, 1000, 2000 or 20 000?

(The answers are after the references.)

some ways there is no need to separate zero from the other numbers for special discussion as it shares the same properties. Sometimes, however, it is easy to overlook. You do not start counting from zero, for example. Moreover, although it represents the empty set, it is *not* nothing. If it were nothing how could it possibly play such an important role in such large sums of money as £ 1 000 000?

In brief, be sure to include work on zero in your early years teaching!

## Concluding remarks

It was not by chance that I opted to discuss place value as the first topic in this book. As a concept it takes years to master, and a lack of appreciation of the complexities involved in the teaching and learning of it result in all manner of problems in later life. If we can begin to understand some of the potential difficulties, however, I think we can go a long way towards ameliorating them. Before I do you might like to do a private check to ensure your understanding of place value. Do not panic if you make an error but, instead, take stock and perhaps do some of the further reading listed below.

## References

DICKSON, L., BROWN, M. and GIBSON, O. (1984) *Children Learning Mathematics*, London: Cassell.

GELMAN, R. and GALLISTEL, C.R. (1978) *The Child's Understanding of Number*, Cambridge, Mass.: Harvard University Press.

HAYLOCK, D. (1995) *Primary Mathematics Explained for Teachers*, London: Paul Chapman Publishing.

HAYLOCK, D. and COCKBURN, A. (1997) *Understanding Mathematics in the Lower Primary Years*, London: Paul Chapman Publishing.

HUGHES, M. (1986) *Children and Number*, Oxford: Blackwell.

KAMII, C. (1985) *Young Children Reinvent Arithmetic*, New York: Teachers College Press.

**Answers:** (1) $\frac{1}{100}$ (2) 2000

# Chapter 3    Why is place value so challenging to teach?

In the Spring 1997, a group of a dozen first and primary school teachers and I sat down and brainstormed all the reasons we found place value challenging to teach. Frequently we concluded that one of the roots of the problem was language but, thinking that was rather vague, we committed ourselves to being as specific as we could possibly be. The efforts of our labours are shown in Figure 3.1 BUT, *before you look*, I suggest you jot down why you think place value is so challenging to teach. (It may be, of course, that you do not, in which case please can you let us in on the secret!)

I asked you to write down your thoughts for two reasons. The first is that you may come up with many more ideas than we did. Secondly, and perhaps more importantly, this book is about encouraging people to unravel the complexities of a topic for themselves. I ***could*** have written a book which analysed all the mathematical topics commonly taught in primary schools in the same way. This would have produced a good fat book and by the end of it you might have had a little more knowledge but, I would argue, you would not be so well equipped as you are likely to be should you make it to the end of this one.

More specifically, this book is designed to encourage you to think, not only of the mathematical complexities of a subject, but also of children's lives and their experiences inside and outside of the classroom. Moreover it will help you focus on

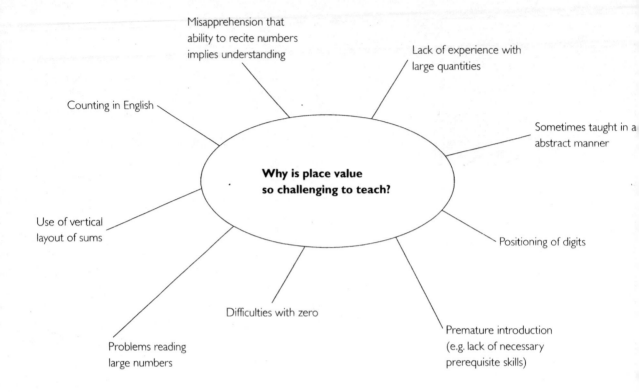

Misapprehension that ability to recite numbers implies understanding

Lack of experience with large quantities

Counting in English

Sometimes taught in a abstract manner

**Why is place value so challenging to teach?**

Use of vertical layout of sums

Positioning of digits

Difficulties with zero

Premature introduction (e.g. lack of necessary prerequisite skills)

Problems reading large numbers

**FIG 3.1**
**Potential difficulties in teaching place value**

your own subject knowledge and professional practice and ponder on how they might influence the way in which you teach a particular topic. Such an approach will enable you to analyse new — as yet, perhaps, unforeseen — components in the primary mathematics curriculum. And, finally, I would argue that the analytical process is far from being simply an academic exercise: indeed, I would go so far as to say that by adopting such an approach you will become a far more effective teacher of primary mathematics.

Figure 3.1 illustrates the potential difficulties in teaching place value the teachers and I came up with. I will explain them briefly and then, later in the chapter, I will provide some suggestions for counteracting the problems.

## Counting in English

If you stop to think about it counting in English may well be confusing for young children: how is one supposed to remember that *'seventeen'* is a smaller number than *'seventy'* when they both begin with 'seven'? What on earth do 'eleven' and 'twelve' mean when the spoken words bear no obvious relationship to any other numbers? It is little wonder that some children have difficulty writing numbers between ten and twenty. The Welsh seem to have adopted a far more sensible approach.

1   un
2   dau (f. dwy)
3   tri (f. tair)
⋮
10 deg
11 un–deg–un
12 un–deg–dau
13 un–deg–tri

## Misapprehension that an ability to recite numbers implies understanding

A fairly common problem among inexperienced student-teachers and some parents is the belief that if children can reel off the numbers one to twenty then they must know what they mean. The fact that this is not necessarily the case was vividly brought home to me several years ago when Sam, a very bright eyed, confident 5-year-old was driving his teacher to distraction: he would spend ages reciting the numbers one to a hundred and had little difficulty in finding a card with '100' on it. If asked to lay out two cubes, however, he looked at her blankly: laying out one cube was no problem but putting out two was apparently beyond him. (Incidentally she did try other strategies in case he did not understand her request but they too failed.)

## Lack of experience

When children are first learning to count, people are all too ready to produce counters, pencils, cubes and so on to aid the process. As the numbers become bigger, however, the props tend to become fewer. Thus, for example, while a child may be

**FIG 3.2**
Gaining experience of
larger numbers

able to count to forty-seven, it is unlikely that they will
rarely — if ever — have knowingly seen forty-seven items (see
Figure 3.2). This does not explain Sam's problem above but
it may be an indication as to why, for example, some children
think 'thirty-*nine*' is bigger than 'forty-*one*' or why some have
very little appreciation of the fact that 'eighty-three pencils'
are considerably more than 'twenty-seven'.

## Abstract teaching

Leinhardt and Putnam (1987) produced a very vivid
description of a teacher working on place value with her
pupils. Here is an edited extract:

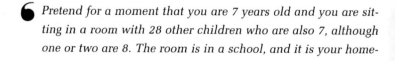

*Pretend for a moment that you are 7 years old and you are sit-
ting in a room with 28 other children who are also 7, although
one or two are 8. The room is in a school, and it is your home-*

*room. . . . Today the teacher is walking around to each of the desks and giving children Popsicle sticks. . . . As the teacher comes to your desk, you can see that there are loose sticks in the orange can and bundles of sticks with rubber bands around them in the blue and purple can. You like blue and purple better than orange, so you take four of the Popsicle stick bundles. . . . At the next desk the teacher asks for 8 sticks. Your neighbor, Baron, looks puzzled. He has two bundles of 10 sticks and 6 loose sticks. . . . There is a long pause; the teacher stands and smiles. . . . Finally, she says, "Can anyone help Baron out?" One of the bolder girls says, "Take the gum band off." You think that is a kind of stupid answer because why would you put all those gum bands on if you were supposed to take them off. . . .* (pp. 557–8)

Whenever I show the account to my students they nod their heads for it all too readily brings back memories of their early struggles with place value.

It seems to me that bundling units into tens is, in theory, a good idea as it develops the notion of exchange. For young children to do so simply because the teacher has instructed them thus, however, seems to be a fairly mindless activity. How are they to remember whether there are to be nine, or ten, or even eleven in a bundle? And, even if they do remember, so what?

FIG 3.3
Counting in tens with meaning

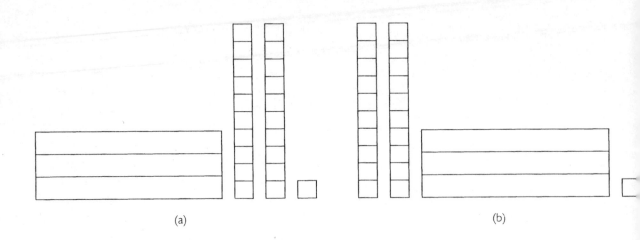

(a)                                                                 (b)

**FIG 3.4**
Dienes blocks representing 3 2 1

When teaching place value I prefer to use everyday objects and involve pupils in meaningful tasks (see Figure 3.3). That is not to say that certain structural apparatus — such as Dienes Multibase Blocks — cannot play an important role in helping children understanding the concepts involved. Pimm (1995) cautions, however, that such equipment should be used with care for it does not represent all of the concepts involved in place value. For example, conventionally, one would show 321 as in Figure 3.4a but there is no real reason why it should not be represented as in Figure 3.4b which might suggest to the child that tens come before hundreds come before units resulting in a number two tens, three hundred and one. In other words, while positioning may be irrelevant to Dienes, it is certainly not the case for place value.

## Position of digit

Earlier in the chapter we considered the notion that children might find it hard to appreciate the quantities represented by large numbers and hence, for example, that 'thirty-nine' was less than 'forty-one'. In part it may well be a lack of experience of working with large quantities is the reason. It may also be because they have not learnt to appreciate that the positioning of a digit is critical when ascertaining the value of a numeral. The nine in '39' may well be the largest digit of the collection under consideration (i.e. 3, 9, 4 and 1) **when thought of in isolation** away from the three but not when positioned after the three and compared to '41': it is not called 'place value' for nothing! Further complexities related to this notion are considered in the following sections.

## Premature introduction

Constance Kamii (1985) is adamant that we introduce children to the idea of place value far too soon in their mathematical careers. She argues that, in the early years of schooling, children have more than enough to do appreciating the cardinality and ordinality of the numbers up to ten. They are, for example, still learning that the numerical difference between four and five is the same as the difference between eight and nine. This being so, it seems a conceptually very tall order to expect them to realise that the difference between forty and fifty is the same as between eighty and ninety.

Related to the notion of premature introduction is Hughes' (1986) view that young children do not necessarily see the value of using conventional written symbols. Thus, perhaps it is not surprising that a child relied on 'dots in her head' (Hughes, 1986, p. 126) rather than figures when calculating twelve minus seven. She only wrote the sum down when encouraged to do so, not because she considered the process of being of any value. It may be that until children are comfortable with conventional number symbols they will find it difficult manipulating larger numbers.

## Zero

Zero seems to be fraught with potential problems! Here are some but I suspect you can quickly come up with others.

Last term, one of my students pointed out that it was all very well talking about zero money meaning no money but how on earth do you equate this to zero temperature: you cannot have no temperature! This led on to a discussion of the variety of words that are used when referring to the symbol '0' — 'nothing', 'naught', 'nil', and of course, as one student said, 'The letter "o" '. I must confess that I have never seen a child confusing the letter and the number but I would not be surprised if someone did make such a mistake especially if a task involved the use of both.

Another major problem I want to discuss in this section is the use of zero as a place holder. As discussed, some children seem to have problems enough with the concept of place value: imagine their added confusion if their conception of zero is 'nothing'. Various researchers and mathematicians have written about this problem but one of the most comprehensive accounts is in Dickson, Brown and Gibson (1984). They cite various cases of children saying, for example, that 10024 is 'one hundred and twenty-four' or that 'thirty-five' is written '305'.

## Reading large numbers

Learning to read in English involves adapting the convention of moving your eyes from left to right across a page. Reading large numbers involves the same convention, however if the number is very large, then a process of grouping the digits *starting from the righthand side* is required. When I was at school we had commas to help us, now we have spaces but, nevertheless, the same process is involved. Try reading 6498261580, for example, without grouping the digits from the right beforehand!

## Vertical layout

The final problem I wish to discuss on the subject of place value is not universal. In the UK we have a tendency to present children with tens and units sums in a vertical layout thus:

$$
\begin{array}{r}
61 \\
-47 \\
\hline
\end{array}
$$

Ultimately, as adults, we may find this format helpful but, for children, it can create a multitude of problems. One of the most common of these is the fact that the symbols are not interpreted as intended. Thus, taking the sum above, a child might take one from seven (thinking you always take the

smaller number from the bigger) and then subtract four from six: sixty-one and forty-seven do not get a look in! Or, if presented with, 419
$$+\underline{206}$$

you may have any one of the following answers:

'22' (i.e. $4 + 1 + 9 + 2 + 0 + 6$)

'615' (i.e. adding the numbers correctly but forgetting to carry the ten of 15)

'625' (correct!)

'213' (i.e. $419 - 206$)

6115' (i.e. after adding nine and six writing '15' and then proceeding correctly)

or even, in an extreme cases, '4' (i.e. $4 + 1 + 9 + 2 + 0 + 6 = 22 = 2 + 2 = 4$) or '6' (i.e. as there are six digits)

## Some thoughts on brainstorming

Obviously I would be curious to know what you jotted down when dwelling on the complexities of place value but as stated in the introduction that is not what this book is about. Rather it is about the *processes* involved in unravelling the potential difficulties when teaching and learning a subject. In this section therefore we will focus on where our ideas might have originated. Looking at the above discussion you will see that my ideas came from:

■ a knowledge of the mathematical concept;

■ observations of, and conversations with, children;

■ discussions with teachers;

■ my work with students;

■ my experiences as a teacher and learner;

■ references to the literature;

■ my knowledge of teaching methods in the UK and abroad.

Some of these sources are perhaps more readily available to me than to you but others will be less so. The crucial point, however, is that I have endeavoured to gain insight into the challenges surrounding the teaching and learning of place value from a variety of perspectives. I read somewhere that brainstorming expands people's thinking and helps them come up with ideas which might not be arrived at by rational methods. That is not to say that my ideas — or your's — are not rational; simply that the process of unearthing them might not have been!

Obviously it would be unrealistic of me to suggest that you, as busy professionals, rush around reading all you can lay your hands on and discussing place value with all and sundry. Rather, I am advocating that when you contemplate the teaching of a new mathematical concept you take a few steps back and spend a little time considering the topic from a mathematical perspective; from a young child's point of view; from your own experience as a teacher and a learner and from anything you might have read or heard on the subject. Better still — if you have time — is to supplement the above with discussion with colleagues and even other adults particularly if they consider themselves to be poor at mathematics.

Brainstorming as a member of a group or on your own will not always uncover the roots of a problem but it is likely to highlight potential pitfalls and, with luck, it will bring to mind some ideas for remedial or even preventative, action. This will be discussed in more detail in Chapter 4.

## Implications for action

As you brainstormed the complexities of place value and read the above you might have begun to devise strategies to reduce the likelihood of problems occurring in the first place. You might also have thought that many of the problems are interrelated. For example, if children were more aware of the significance of the positioning of digits, they might have fewer problems with the vertical layout of sums. Or, if children counted large quantities more frequently, they might have more of an appreciation of the relative size of numbers.

Thus just as the problems are interrelated, so too are the solutions but, as I presented the complexities as specific problems, I will now discuss some specific solutions. Strategies for one potential problem might equally well help minimise another. I am not suggesting that the ideas are by any means exhaustive nor am I proposing that you try them all, but, I can assure you, they have been tried and tested.

## Language difficulties

There is no getting away from the fact that counting in English can be tricky for beginners but, rather than ignore the issue or skate over it, I would emphasise it. It is rather like recognising that 'i's and 'e's together can make for spelling complications but, knowing that, one makes an extra effort.

I have heard it suggested that rather than using the conventional number system to introduce the teens, you use words such as 'oneteen' (11), 'twoteen' (12) and so on. Although I have not tried it and can see some advantages, I personally have a feeling that it might be a bit like the Initial Teaching Alphabet (ITA) was for readers: fine for the able children who had little need for it but not so fine for the less able who had to learn ITA letters and *then* learn another set of conventional letters.

A game I have found very helpful and popular is 'Find the number'. Basically someone thinks of a number between, for example, one and twenty and, by asking a series of 'yes/no' questions, others have to determine the number. Not only is it an enjoyable exercise but it is also a useful diagnostic tool as the type of questions soon indicate the depth of understanding: 'Is it more than ten?' and 'Is it odd?' being rather more sophisticated than 'Is it six?' when it comes to the first questions.

Traditional songs, stories and rhymes are also useful as are more home-spun varieties produced by the class. And, of course, constant practise be it formal or informal: reciting the numbers for the sake of it or counting out the dinner numbers and so on.

## Counting with meaning rather than recitation

There are whole tomes such as the elderly, but very detailed, Gelman and Gallistel (1978) on teaching children how to count meaningfully. Some of this has been effectively summarised by Montague-Smith (1997). It would be inappropriate for me to launch into all the recommended strategies here. Suffice it to say two things. The first is that some parents and novice adult helpers might require a little gentle education especially if the children they have observed have had no apparent difficulties. For example, you might introduce a discussion on the complexities of counting (as considered in the last chapter) to demonstrate that the recitation of numbers does not necessarily imply the ability to count. My second point is that I think children need interesting and child-relevant activities: counting the individuals for hot dinners is fine as an exemplar but I suspect, left to their own devices, most children would gain more from counting out balloons for a party or balls for a game.

## Working with larger quantities

The activities above could easily be extended to larger quantities but one would need to be careful that the counting out did not become too long and tedious! A more interesting and challenging activity could be to compare two bundles of cubes and guess which would build the taller tower. The children could guess the number in each pile, build the towers and see whose guess was most accurate.

You might also try comparing different types of items such as counters and cubes. The results could be interesting; for those unfamiliar with Piaget and his critics, take care of how you phrase the questions. For example, asking if there are more cubes (of which there are 10) or counters (of which there are 15) might elicit the response, 'cubes' as the child is focusing on the volume of the objects rather than their quantity.

## Making meaning

Classrooms are full of wonderful items to count but, the problems described by Leinhardt and Putnam (1987), are not just the result of making a rather dull choice. The more fundamental points are that the task had no framework or interest for the children. Now if they had been packing pencils into boxes as shown in Figure 3.3 (p. 32) then the exercise might have been more meaningful and hence more successful.

My colleague, Derek Haylock, is a firm advocate of using money to assist the idea of exchange and place value. I can see the beauty of using such ready-made everyday materials but a word of caution: you must be convinced that the children are ready for the experience as within a class of six-year-olds you can have some who are happy with spending a fortune and handling change. In contrast others may see any coin as having a value of 'one' in the same way as counters — regardless of colour and size — have always been referred to as 'one'. Once children begin to appreciate that different coins have different values they may then find the fact that a 5p is smaller than a 2p difficult to cope with.

Calculators can prove a very useful tool in demonstrating the importance of place in value. Most will be familiar with the idea of adding a series of tens to, for example, 3 and encouraging the children to predict the next number on the calculator. Similarly tens can be used to subtract, multiply or even divide. To add an extension — and perhaps a little more interest — to the activity one can play 'Place Invaders'. Children generally play in pairs and are presented with a sheet each such as shown in Figure 3.5. From then the game is really self-explanatory with the children taking it in turns to predict which buttons to press.

| enter | wipe out | keys pressed | display | score |
|-------|----------|--------------|---------|-------|
| 431   | 3        | −30          | 401     | 1     |
| 24    | 4        |              |         |       |
| 849   | 8        |              |         |       |
| 206   | 6        |              |         |       |

G 3.5
ace Invaders

FIG 3.6
Place building

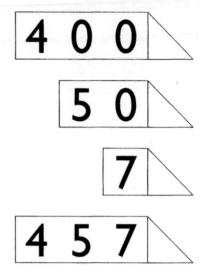

There is a wide variety of computer activities which can assist in building up an appreciation of place value but I am not even going to name them as (1) they are easy to find and (2) naming them would date the book faster than anything else!

While technology can be invaluable, I would also recommend a more home-spun approach by building up numbers as suggested by Hopkins et al. (1996). As shown in Figure 3.6, you simply have a set of unit cards, with a set of units (0–9), a set of tens (10–90), a set of hundreds (100–900) and so on, from which you can build any number from '0' to '999'!

A similar idea is to draw a rectangle around numbers to be added. For example if a rectangle were drawn around 326 and another around 210 then a child is more likely to perceive them as two large numbers in the hundreds rather than six separate digits (increasing the likelihood of 536 as an answer instead of 14!).

Games have also been found to be an effective way to increase children's knowledge and understanding of place value (Cockburn and Pettitt, 1987; Kamii, 1985). These can be commercially produced but, personally, I prefer the home-made variety. The latter tending to be more focused on specific concepts rather than concerned with distracting rules (e.g. throw a six to start) and requiring a range of operations (e.g. number recognition, addition and subtraction).

Menne (1996/97) describes a game which can be fun to do as a class. The children are presented with a folder, such as Figure 3.7. One of the windows is open to reveal a number. The children's task is to discover the number hidden behind the other window which, coupled with the digit in view will make up the teacher's age. That may be fine when the teacher is '27' but I suspect I might adapt the game in my forties and fifties to how many pencils were in my cupboard!

FIG 3.7
Menne's guessing game

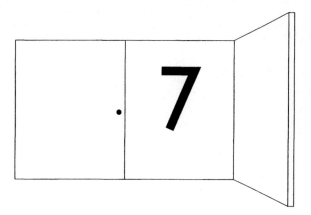

Given the complexity of place value my advice is to wait until a child is ready to embark on it. That is not to say that there is no mention of numbers over nine in the classroom but rather that they should be part of the background rather than a major part of the mathematics curriculum in the early years.

## References

COCKBURN, A.D. and PETTITT, D. (1987) 'Planning mathematical games in the infant school', *Times Educational Supplement*, 2 October.

DICKSON, L., BROWN, M. and GIBSON, O. (1984) *Children Learning Mathematics*, London, Cassell.

GELMAN, R. and GALLISTEL, C.R. (1978) *The Child's Understanding of Number*, Cambridge, Mass., Harvard University Press.

HOPKINS, C., GIFFORD, S. and PEPPERELL, S. (1996) *Mathematics in the Primary School*, London, David Fulton Publishers.

HUGHES, M. (1986) *Children and Number*, Oxford, Blackwell.

KAMII, C. (1985) *Young Children Reinvent Arithmetic*, New York, Teachers' College Press.

LEINHARDT, G. and PUTNAM, R.T. (1987) 'The skill of learning from classroom lessons', *American Educational Research Journal*, **24**, pp. 557–87.

MENNE, J. (1996/97) 'Hoe oud is de juf?', *Willem Bartjens*, **16**, pp. 9– 11.

MONTAGUE-SMITH, A. (1997) *Mathematics in Nursery Education*, London, David Fulton Publishers.

PIMM, D. (1995) *Symbols and Meanings in School Mathematics*, London, Routledge.

# Chapter 4    Exploring the analytical process in greater depth

In Chapter 3 I introduced a brainstorming technique to explore some of the potential difficulties associated with place value. I could, of course, have opted to write a book where all the topics in a typical mathematics curriculum were analysed, saving you the time and energy of reading this chapter. I decided not to for three reasons. The first is frivolous in so far as, at the moment, I feel that my mathematical knowledge is insufficient to cope with such a challenge. Lest you say the same applies to you, be assured that I have suggestions for resolving that particular difficulty!

The second reason for explaining the process lies at the heart of the reason for writing this book: it is my belief that to be a really effective teacher one not only needs to know one's subject but one needs to be able to view it, and appreciate it, from a range of perspectives. Certainly I could produce a detailed analysis of the complexities of addition, money, multiplication, fractions, area and so on but, as many — especially those of a certain generation or older — have discovered to their cost, learning to use something such as a computer effectively, requires plenty of personal experience. You can read about a topic until you are cross-eyed but, even if that does not tie your brain in knots, it almost certainly does little to assist your mastery.

The third reason for the lack of a series of diagrams, such as Figure 3.1 (p. 28), is that the world of mathematics is changing

— albeit it slowly — but, nonetheless, the subject as it is taught in schools is evolving. This makes it impossible to produce a diagram which will be appropriate for ever more. Gone are the logarithms I was taught in the early years of secondary school while games and investigations were unheard of in the mathematics classroom twenty or thirty years ago.

Below I have outlined some steps which I hope will help you in the brainstorming technique I am advocating. Before I do so however, I should point out that I do not necessarily see your brainstorming as a ten minute, 'jot down all you can think of' activity as it is usually described. If that is all you have time for then fine. That alone should provide you with some valuable insights. If you have longer, however, you can do a quick brainstorm of initial ideas, have a think, read, observation, chat or whatever and return to your original jottings several days later. With a bit of practice such an approach is likely to be both illuminating and worthwhile: not only will it give you a greater appreciation of the complexities of a topic, it is also likely to direct you to strategies for reducing the likelihood of potential problems.

## Step 1: Unravelling the mathematical complexities of a topic

As numerate adults I suspect the vast majority of us take our mathematical knowledge for granted when it comes to teaching young children. Schemes and colleagues are there to guide us if we are a little rusty about the fine detail but, for the most part, I would suggest that we are all fairly confident of our ability to teach a mathematical topic. Certainly, for some, this may well be true. The problem for the majority of us, however is that we do not know what we do not know because we do not know of its existence! You could, argue 'so where is the problem?' but, as Haylock and Cockburn (1997) state, you might — albeit unwittingly — be creating difficulties for your pupils in later life. Take, for example, the case of 'taking away': if children are only taught that subtraction involves taking away then they can experience real difficulties when confronted with 'the difference between' or those baffling missing number sums such as '? + 2 = 6'. Indeed they could end up like me not knowing why, as my teacher taught me 'two minuses make a plus'! (The answer is in the next chapter should you be interested.)

Part of the solution lies in finding a comprehensive and comprehensible mathematics book which outlines the concepts you are likely to teach in detail. As one who has made several expensive mistakes, I suggest you look very closely at the book and the author's credentials before you buy it or borrow it from the library. Nowadays I usually opt for books written by mathematicians so that I can be secure in the knowledge that they know their mathematics BUT — and this is vitally important — it is crucial that I also understand what they are talking about! I like to think I am reasonably intelligent but the number of times I have been put off by mathematicians rushing through topics leaving me far behind is embarrassingly large! At the end of this chapter I have listed some books that I have found accessible and helpful but, before you dart out and buy them, check them out: they may not be written in a style which suits you and your particular needs. Sometimes, if you are teaching a specific topic or you have a child with an unusual complex problem, you may require a specialist book on, for example, measurement or probability. There are plenty about but you may well need to go to a large bookshop with, ideally, mathematics and education sections.

The time has passed when the majority of educationalists behaved as if children were empty vessels who had to be filled with knowledge. Increasing your own mathematical knowledge therefore is no longer enough hence Step 2 . . .

## Step 2: Considering psychological complexities

In Chapter 10 I will be discussing some of the psychological issues of being a pupil in a classroom situation, but here I want to explore some of the potential psychological problems related to understanding mathematics.

The first is, of course, that some people hate mathematics! The usual reasons for this seem to be a fear of being wrong, bad 'press' from parents and an inability — which I hasten to add, is not innate — to see the relevance of the subject. As educators, we obviously do what we can to alleviate these feelings by making activities as intrinsically interesting as possible although, as will be discussed in more detail in Chapter 10, it is sometimes hard to disguise the fact that you are, in effect, the director of classroom proceedings. This can create problems even in some of your most motivating and interesting sessions if you are not careful for, as one teacher friend complained to me,

> ❝ . . . something that is always there is what does she want and that's the thing you are trying for them not to do . . . because they are operating in such a large group, you are the person who is dictating what is going to happen and, obviously, that is the major thing that is going on in the classroom: what does she want.

Being aware of the above is a very useful start but how else can you unravel some of the potential psychological problems prior to teaching a topic? You can make good use of the strategies described below but you can also consider your own response to the teaching and learning of certain topics. For example, what are your views on the learning of multiplication tables? I think we would all agree that it is useful to know them off by heart but it is potentially a rather arid task and, like it or not, there is no avoiding that you are either right or wrong when it comes to answering $8 \times 7 = \square$. Again I would suggest that having this insight can help you adopt appropriate actions.

Or, for example, consider weighing two objects of different density: one is very large but is not at all dense (e.g. a bag of feathers) and the other is a very small but very dense (e.g. a piece of lead). There are mathematical issues to be discussed here but there are also psychological ones when coming to terms with the idea that visual perceptions can sometimes be misleading.

## Step 3: Teacher observation

There was a time when there was sufficient money — and enlightenment — in schools and local education authorities to

FIG 4.1
Capturing your every move

allow teachers to observe one another. Unfortunately, at time
of writing, there is little enough money for books in most
schools let alone any left over for something as worthwhile
as the professional development which comes from
observing others.

Be that as it may, do watch others when you can but
also observe yourself. I do not mean by having video
cameras and microphones to capture your every move for later
analysis (Figure 4.1). Rather you might discreetly tape-record
your mathematics sessions from time to time. I have often
encouraged students to do that in the past and they are almost
invariably amazed by what they hear. This tends to be
particularly true when they are monitoring their behaviour
towards girls and boys: their general belief beforehand is that
there will be no difference but, in reality, that is rarely the
case. (Writers such as Elizabeth Fennema and Hilary Shuard
have much to say on mathematics and gender.)

It may be that tape recording – or even just reflecting on the
type of errors your pupils typically make – will draw your
attention to aspects of your behaviour which rather than
promoting mathematical thinking may be hindering it. Take
the case of Jane. She had a set phrase for describing addition
sums: 'Six add four makes ten'; 'Three add two makes five';
and so on. She frequently found that her pupils had difficulty
with the equals sign when it came to subtraction: she had
never explained what it meant in general terms and her pupils

had problems with understanding how 'making' — rather than destructing — was involved in 'taking away'. (Shoecraft, 1989, has produced an interesting article on the equals sign which is referenced at the end of this chapter.)

## Step 4: Child observation and discussion

Classrooms are extremely busy and vibrant environments. They are full of people with their own ideas and interpretations and you can be sure that when you are explaining a mathematical concept there will almost invariably be one child who picks up the wrong end of the stick. This is not to imply that your explanation is faulty or that the child is not very able. Indeed it can often be the more intelligent and thoughtful children who may jump to the wrong conclusions. This idea will be taken up again in Chapter 10 but in the meantime let us consider an example taken from Cockburn (1992):

> *Paul was doing some work on floating and sinking when his teacher presented him with one of those plastic, practise golf balls with holes in it.*
>
> *Teacher: If we put this in water do you think it will float or sink?*
> *Paul:     Sink.*
> *Teacher: Why?*
> *Paul:     Because the water will go into the holes.*
> *Teacher: What would happen if I wrapped it in clingfilm?*
> *Paul:     What's clingfilm?*
> *Teacher: It's the stuff you wrap your sandwiches in.*
> *Paul:.    It would sink.*
>
> *Now the conversation could have ended there with the teacher assuming that Paul did not really understand the concepts of floating and sinking. However it went on:*
> *Teacher: Why do you say that?*
> *Paul:     Because the weight of the sandwiches would have weighed it down.*                    (pp. 19–20)

Watching children at work can be highly illuminating but it can be extremely difficult not to jump in when you see them making mistakes. As a student-teacher I was taught to teach not to observe: it was very hard to break the habit. The same was found by Bennett, Desforges, Cockburn and Wilkinson (1984) when they tried to encourage teachers to watch their pupils at work. Unfortunately, jumping in to help is usually the wrong approach as it tends to hide the underlying problem. Thus, although you might have a resolution in the short term, the problem is likely to recur when you are not watching. It is better, if you can, to follow the advice of a local teacher, Mary,

> ❝ *I try to get to where it first broke down. There is no point in concreting over the cracks.*

Talking over mathematical problems with children can also be invaluable. The tendency to talk '*to*' or '*at*' rather than '*with*' should be avoided if at all possible (even when you are pulling your hair out). Again this is not as easy as it sounds especially if the children are young for, as will be discussed further in Chapter 10, they often find it hard to articulate their thinking. Nevertheless, Mason (1987) urges us to try

> ❝ *. . . to enter a student's world (mostly by listening) rather than trying to always drag them into our inner mathematical world.*
>
> (p. 80)

He goes on to explain the importance of

> ❝ *. . . taking opportunities for listening to students to get them talking because transition from seeing to saying is a necessary part of the struggle towards meaning . . . it is in the act of expressing to others that we often gain clarity for ourselves.*
>
> (p. 80)

Finally it is worth watching your children in the playground from time to time or even asking someone else to do it for, or with, you. Rather than just noting whether they are behaving themselves or not, try to stand back and see how you might observe for the first time. I have found children who are very quiet and seemingly not very able in the classroom take on an entirely different persona in the playground becoming highly articulate and intelligent ring leaders: where does that leave the next stage of their mathematics education?

## Step 5: Discussions with adults

Although you may not have the chance to observe them
teaching, I would certainly hope that you have a chance to
have professional dialogues with your colleagues. These serve
all manner of functions (including blowing your top when
Rachel has poured sand and glue down the sink yet again!)
Here I would particularly like to suggest that you find a quiet
ten minutes or so — when you are not exhausted at the end
of the day — to encourage your colleagues to join in the
brainstorming process with you. Not only are they likely to act
as a catalyst for your thinking but they may well come up with
some ideas of potential problems and, indeed, if you are lucky,
you may all find the experience intellectually stimulating.

Should you decide to adopt a group brainstorming approach
I suggest you set four simple ground rules beforehand,
otherwise you may discourage your more sensitive colleagues
from opening their mouths and dampen any creativity likely to
surface among you and your colleagues. Before a brainstorming
session I have found it helpful to explain that

1  suggestions may be called out in any order (they can be
   sorted later if necessary but it can stop the flow if you have
   to process them during the brainstorming);
2  no explanations or justifications are required (clarifications
   can come later if necessary);
3  all suggestions that spring to mind — however trivial or
   stupid they may seem in the first instance — should not
   be censored as;
4  all participants will refrain from commenting on other
   people's suggestions!

## Step 6: Researching the literature

I probably should not admit this in such a public arena
but I find some of the research literature dull, tedious and
impenetrable! Having said that, some of it I find very exciting
and, believe it or not, I want to tell everyone about my new
pieces of knowledge: whether the recipients — i.e. my students
— find the research I refer to throughout this book so
fascinating I am not so sure . . .

Earlier in the chapter I suggested that you might find it helpful to buy a basic mathematics book. I am not suggesting you necessarily buy numerous books by researchers, although there are some notable exceptions, in my view, worth purchasing rather than borrowing from the library. Margaret Donaldson's (1978) *Children's Minds* is a classic, for example, as is Martin Hughes' (1986) *Children and Number*. At the risk of sounding conceited, I should also add that I have been told that Desforges and Cockburn's (1987) *Understanding the Mathematics Teacher* is very readable.

You may well question what researchers — some of whom have not taught for years — might have to offer you, a busy teacher with too many children in your class and too little money to provide for them adequately. As I hope will be obvious from this book, reading of others' research can provide a valuable source of intellectual stimulation; it can stop you falling into a despondent rut as you are surrounded by yet more demands and, from the point of view of this book, it can provide you with valuable insights into children's mathematical thinking. For example, did you know that children tend to learn some doubles facts (e.g. 2 + 2, 5 + 5 and 3 + 3) sooner than they do adding one to numbers such as six and four (i.e. 6 + 1, 1 + 6, 4 + 1 and 1 + 4) (Kamii, 1985). Or that some teachers respond rather differently to boys and girls in mathematics sessions (see, for example, Burton, 1989).

A good place to start finding research literature which might be of interest is to look at the references at the end of each chapter in this book. If you cannot find them in your local library or, if when you locate them they are not to your taste, do not be put off: the fact that you have read this far in this book suggests that it will not be long before you find something of interest which will promote your thinking on teaching mathematics with insight.

## Concluding remarks

I hope you will find the techniques discussed in this chapter helpful. I would like to urge you to give them all a try, bearing in mind that there may well be other ways to further your thoughts on the complexities of teaching mathematics to young children which you might also wish to explore. One of the beauties of using such a brainstorming technique is that preventative measures often present themselves so that rather than waiting for errors to occur you can reduce the likelihood of them happening in the first place.

# References

BENNETT, N., DESFORGES, C., COCKBURN, A. and WILKINSON, B. (1984) *The Quality of Pupil Learning Experiences*, London, Lawrence Erlbaum Associates.

BURTON, L. (1989) 'Images of mathematics', in ERNEST, P. (ed.) *Mathematics: The State of the Art*, London, Falmer Press.

COCKBURN, A.D. (1992) *Beginning Teaching*, London, Paul Chapman Publishing.

DESFORGES, C. and COCKBURN, A. (1987) *Understanding the Mathematics Teacher*, London, Falmer Press.

* DICKSON, L., BROWN, M. and GIBSON, O. (1984) *Children Learning Mathematics*, London, Cassell.

DONALDSON, M. (1978) *Children's Minds*, London, Fontana.

* HAYLOCK, D. and COCKBURN, A. (1997) *Understanding Mathematics in the Lower Primary Years*, London, Paul Chapman Publishing.

* HOPKINS, C., GIFFORD, S. and PEPPERELL, S. (1996) *Mathematics in the Primary School*, London, David Fulton Publishers.

HUGHES, M. (1986) *Children and Number*, Oxford, Blackwell.

KAMII, C. (1985) *Young Children Reinvent Arithmetic*, New York, Teachers' College Press.

MASON, J. (1987) 'What do symbols represent?', in JANVIER, C. (ed.) *Problems of Representation in the Teaching and Learning of Mathematics*, Hillsdale, N.J., Lawrence Erlbaum Associates.

SHOECRAFT, P. (1989) '"Equals" means "is the same as"', *Arithmetic Teacher*, April, pp. 36–40.

* THYER, D. and MAGGS, J. (1991) *Teaching Mathematics to Young Children* (*3rd edn*), London, Cassell.

* WILLIAMS, E. and SHUARD, H. (1994) *Primary Mathematics Today* (*4th edn*), Harlow, Longman.

* Books marked with an asterisk are basic mathematics books which my students and I have found particularly helpful.

# Chapter 5

# What is subtraction?

Subtraction is one of those topics which, I suspect, most of us think we have mastered from a very early age. Six take away four is two: what could be easier? Oh that it were so simple!

For many years I thought I knew pretty well all there was to know about subtraction. There was a slight hiatus when I came across negative numbers but I soon picked up the idea that, 'Two minuses make a plus' (For those unfamiliar with this, if you are confronted by two minus signs side by side and you interpret them as a plus, then the correct answer will result. Thus, for example, $6 - (-2) = 8$. (The reasoning behind this should become clear later on the chapter.) It was only, if I am honest, when I became involved in teacher education that I really began to examine the notion of subtraction and, being even more honest, I was appalled by my earlier ignorance. It was not that I found the various forms of subtraction particularly difficult but rather that I had been totally unaware of them. I hope none of my pupils suffered as a result for, as noted in the introduction, if children are misled — albeit unwittingly — into having very narrow, rigid conceptions of a topic, then it can hinder their later mathematical progress (see, for example, Haylock and Cockburn, 1997).

## Some basic concepts

Subtraction comes in many guises. To teach young children about it there are some basic thoughts to keep in mind. Firstly,

FIG 5.1
Using a number line to solve
4 + ? = 7

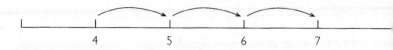

the various forms are not particularly difficult if taken in isolation and, indeed, many young children can tackle at least two forms from an early age without any formal schooling whatsoever. For example, they can do 'take away' tasks if presented in an appropriate manner (Hughes, 1986). They can usually also do 'difference between' tasks if you think about it because they generally know that if you have five sweets and I have four that you have more than I do and they can often tell you by how many.

The second point to remember is that the process of subtraction can sometimes be instigated by symbols other than '−'. For example 4 + ? = 7 may involve subtraction for its solution (especially if you use a calculator.)

Thirdly, however, many subtraction sums can also be solved by other means. Thus, it would have been perfectly valid to solve the above by adding on as shown on the number line in Figure 5.1.

Finally, children need to recognise subtraction in its many forms so that they know which button to press on the calculator!

There are a variety of very good books and articles which outline the intricacies of subtraction in detail (e.g. Dickson, Brown and Gibson, 1984; Haylock and Cockburn, 1997; and Fuson, 1992). Fundamentally, however, subtraction can involve four broad categories of problem.

Ai) *One set* of items such as a set of letters ▨ ▨ ▨ ▨ from which, basically, you remove items. Problems involve comparing the original number of items with the final number. Thus you might start with four letters, remove three and wonder how many letters were left.

*or*

Aii) *One item* such as a pencil ✐ which you do something to — such as shorten through use — and, as above, problems involve before and after comparisons. For example you might have a pencil which is six centimetres long. You write a book and wear away one centimetre of it. How long is it now?

*or*

Bi) *Two sets* of items such as a set of letters ▯ ▯ ▯ ▯
and a set of envelopes ⊠ ⊠ ⊠ which, in essence, you compare in some way: if I have written four letters but only have three envelopes, how many more envelopes do I need?

*or*

Bii) *Two items* such as two pencils ✎ ✎ which, in effect, you compare. For example, Mary's pencil is six centimetres long and Jane's pencil is eight centimetres long, what is the difference in length between the two pencils?

Subtraction problems such as both A types above involve taking away, cutting down, removing in some way as exemplifed in Figure 5.2 where Mrs Brown has just baked eight cakes only to have three of them eaten by her hungry daughter.

Problems of type Ai are common in young children's everyday life and therefore are unlikely to cause conceptual difficulties; however, such problems need to be carefully worded to allow for pupil interpretation. For example, if you present children with,

G 5.2
ype A subtraction problem

**6** *There were six birds on a tree. Two fly away. How many are there now?*

they would be justified in replying, 'Six' for, indeed, there are still six birds: it is just that two of them are no longer on the tree. A more reliable question therefore might be, 'There are si birds on a tree. Two fly away *but none arrive*. How many are *on the tree* now?' (It could be argued that adding the phrases in italics is unnecessary but, if you are trying to cultivate your pupils' imagination in, for example, English sessions, you might end up with a creative response such as 'eight' without them.)

Young children also encounter Aii type situations in their lives but they are less likely to be presented in the context of subtraction. For example, a child might have a hair cut; or a pencil could shorten during the course of a week as a result of great industry; or the level of milk goes down as it is drunk. There are many similarities with type Ai problems but, unless there is a major tragedy (e.g. sweets are eaten, birds killed), type Ai problems frequently can be immediately reversed and returned to their original format whereas type Aii problems generally cannot be with the same effect and immediacy (i.e. hair could be stuck back on or grow but nevertheless the situation will have changed as a result of the subtraction process).

It is important that young children have experience of type Ai and Aii problems *and* that they are correctly represented. This will be discussed in greater detail in the next chapter but, in passing, you might pause to think about a situation which I have seen misleadingly represented on several occasions. A child is presented with a problem such as, 'I have six sweets i a bag. I eat two of them, how many are left?' The problem is then represented using unifix cubes as shown below:

Given this picture it would not be unreasonable for a child to pipe up that there were eight sweets in the problem (rather than just the six in the bag as stated). If the child then has to illustrate the answer you could end up with double the original number of sweets creating all manner of confusion for a thoughtful child.

Moving on to type B problems, however, you can see that the above could be a suitable representation (although your initial reaction — probably due to earlier conditioning — might make you think otherwise). For example, the problem might be, 'If John has six letters and two envelopes, how many more envelopes does he need before he can post his letters?' The number of cubes would then be *compared* (i.e. six with two) and, with luck, the problem solved. Again, requests that the solution should be illustrated are best avoided as they are likely to create misunderstandings.

As with type Ai problems, children frequently encounter type Bi problems in their everyday life and they often have strategies for solving them. For example, they might compare the letters with the envelopes in the paragraph above by matching them one to one.

Children, in my experience frequently compare numbers of sweets informally, and yet, problems involving 'more than', 'fewer than', 'the same as' which are set in school are far less common than those involving taking away items from a single set.

Young children forever seem to be comparing their heights, ages and the size of their pieces of cake. In other words, they have plenty of experience of type Bii problems. These can be more difficult to convert to easily solvable mathematical problems however as, for example, a quarter can have great significance when one is five years three months old making precise whole number subtraction difficult! The problem is exacerbated when one is comparing heights as crucial fractions are also coupled with numbers generally beyond the children's experience e.g. $122^{1}/_{2}$ cm $- 119^{1}/_{4}$ cm $= ?$ Figure 5.3 would represent a type Bii problem if I knew what height to make the mammoths!

Nevertheless, as discussed in the next chapter, young children can gain plenty of experience with the prerequisite skills

FIG 5.3
A potential type Bii problem

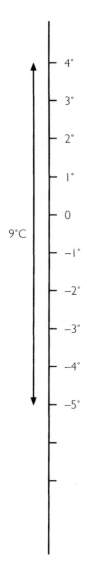

4°
3°
2°
1°
0
9°C
−1°
−2°
−3°
−4°
−5°

FIG 5.4
A 'thermometer' illustrating the
difference in temperature between
4°C and −5°C

necessary for type Bii subtraction. There can, however, be problems when a child is confronted with the notion that they are 'shorter' than someone else but, as will be demonstrated, these are generally not insurmountable.

## Postscript

So have you discovered why 'two minuses make a plus'? Pimm (1995) recounts the tale of a teacher who, when aged ten, reasoned that the '+' sign was made from two '−' signs and therefore it was not surprising that two minuses made a plus (although they could equally well be used to make the '=' sign).

More conventional explanations usually involve giving examples and encouraging individuals to think of the comparison (difference between) form of subtraction: if it was 4°C yesterday and it is −5°C today by how much has the temperature dropped? The answer is $4° − (−5°) = 9°C$, as illustrated in Figure 5.4.

## References

DICKSON, L., BROWN, M. and GIBSON, O. (1984) *Children Learning Mathematics*, London, Cassell.

Fuson, K. (1992) 'Research on whole number addition and subtraction', in Grouws, D.A. (ed.) *Handbook of Research on Mathematics Teaching and Learning*, New York, Macmillan.

Haylock, D. and Cockburn, A.D. (1997) *Understanding Mathematics in the Lower Primary Years*, London, Paul Chapman Publishing.

Hughes, M. (1986) *Children and Number*, Oxford, Blackwell.

Pimm, D. (1995) *Symbols and Meanings in School Mathematics*, London, Routledge.

## Chapter 6    Unravelling the complexities of subtraction

In the previous chapter I described the basic types of subtraction. From this alone it is easy to see why teachers often find subtraction difficult to teach and young children find it difficult to understand.

In this chapter I want to extend the notion of brainstorming using the techniques described in Chapter 3 and further discussed in Chapter 4. As a starting point I suggest you think about the teaching and learning of subtraction and any potential associated problems. Do not worry if you have very little to write but, before you abandon the task, try reflecting on:

■ the different forms of subtraction described in the previous chapter and any related difficulties;
■ your own experiences of learning the subject;
■ any problems you have encountered when teaching subtraction;
■ observations of, and conversations with, pupils at work recalling the type of errors they make and any insights you might have about them;
■ discussions you might have had with colleagues and other adults;
■ anything you might have read about subtraction.

You may be tempted to cheat and have a look at my brainstorming efforts but try not to. You may find that your efforts are far more impressive than mine but, to a certain extent, that is beside the point as this is about developing *you* ability to analyse a topic rather than come up with a complete catalogue of potential problems. Having said that, of course, like any conscientious child I would care to know what ideas you come up with that I overlooked.

Figure 6.1 summarises the thoughts of the teachers' mathematics group when thinking about subtraction. It includes a further stage of analysis to that previously discussed. More specifically, we found it helpful to think in terms of four categories. They are not mutually exclusive and clear cut but I do not see this as a major problem as they are simply tools for unravelling some of the complexities of subtraction. If you find it helpful to add categories do so. If you find it hard to decide which category a problem goes into there is no reason why it cannot go into two or even three. The categories we have found most revealing were:

1   Intrinsic mathematical problems (imp)
2   Intrinsic psychological problems (ipp)
3   Extrinsic home-related problems (ehp)
4   Extrinsic school-related problems (esp)

Below I shall consider examples of each category but, before I do so, you may find it helpful to consider how you are going to record your items in their various categories. You may simply jot down one (or more) of the above sets of initials beside each problem or you may prefer to devise a format such as that shown in Figure 6.1 which, as will become apparent, may be easier to read at a glance.

## Intrinsic mathematical problems

What then is an 'intrinsic mathematical problem (imp)'? One of the basic problems with subtraction is the sheer number of meanings something as seemingly simple as '6 − 4 = 2' can have. For example it represents any one of the following stories:

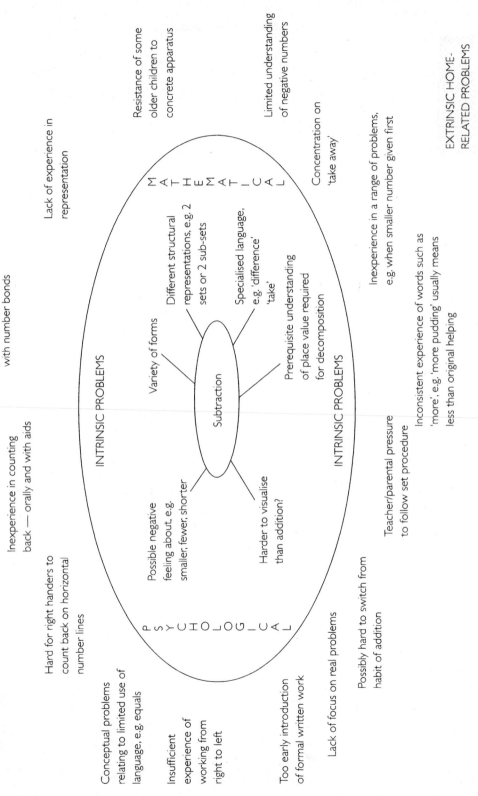

FIG 6.1
Unravelling the complexities of subtraction

- I made 6 cream buns. Sally ate 4 of them. How many buns were left for me?
- I made 6 cream buns. Sally made 4. How many more buns did I make than Sally?
- I made 6 cream buns. Sally made 4. How many fewer buns did Sally make than I?
- I made 6 cream buns. Sally made 4. What is the difference in the number of buns we each made?
- I made 6 cream buns. 4 had white icing on the top. How many did not?
- I made 6 litres of orange juice. Sally drank 4 litres of it. How many litres were left?
- I made 6 litres of orange juice. Sally made 4 litres. How much more did I make than Sally?
- I made 6 litres of orange juice. Sally made 4 litres. How much less did Sally make than I?
- I made 6 litres of orange juice. Sally made 4 litres. What is the difference in the amount we both made?
- I made 6 litres of orange juice. 4 of those litres were made using hot water. How many were not made using hot water?

A basic mathematical fact — and in this instance a potential problem — about subtraction therefore is the sheer variety of forms. As discussed in the previous chapter, for example, an overemphasis on the 'take away' form of subtraction accompanied by little or no mention of the other forms can result in limited understanding which, in the later years of schooling, can inhibit — and possibly even prevent — greater insight into the wider concept of subtraction.

Associated with this potential problem are the different structural representations which can be used when illustrating, for example, '6 − 4 = ?' with objects. Basically one can have **one set** (e.g. of 6 cars) or **an object** (e.g. a six metre hedge) from which four items (e.g. cars) or parts (e.g. metres) are removed or one can have **two sets** (e.g. of 6 and 4 cars) or **two objects** (e.g. hedges) which, in essence, are to be compared.

Another important potential problem which could be classed as 'imp' is the fact that subtraction problems often include specialised language involving words which frequently have other meanings in everyday usage. A common example is the word 'difference'. If people are asked the difference between six green cubes and four red cubes, their likely response will almost certainly be 'colour' rather than 'two'. Stopping to think about it, young children seem to spend quite a lot of time thinking about differences; sometimes it is to do with mathematics (differences in ages, heights, size of cake, etc.) but often it is not (differences in colour, sound, smell, etc.).

Pimm (1995) warns that, as adults, we are often too familiar with words but that,

> Anyone who has struggled to generate expressions in a foreign language in which they are not very fluent will appreciate the reverse situation.　　　　　　　　　　　　　　　　　　(p. 5)

As teachers we must endeavour to be explicit when using everyday words with specialised mathematical meaning. 'Take' is another example which can cause create confusion. To a young child, for example, 'I will take you home' is rather different to, 'six sweets take away four sweets'.

A final imp I wish to consider briefly is that, for subtraction involving numbers over ten, one may need a good understanding of place value. This was considered in more detail in Chapter 2 but, suffice it to say here that, when considering intrinsic mathematical problems it can be important to think of how the lack of prerequisite understanding may hamper further development.

## Intrinsic psychological problems

How often have you observed someone admiring a little old lady and saying 'My, how you have shrunk?' Or how often have you heard a child exclaim, 'My, how lucky I am to have fewer sweets than you?' The answer to both, I suspect, is 'never'. As we point out in our book (Haylock and Cockburn, 1997), there are far more words in the English language describing more, bigger, greater, larger, etc. than there are describing fewer, smaller, etc. Indeed, I would argue, that many people have a psychological bias towards more rather than fewer, taller rather than shorter, and so on. As one gets older there are one or two notable exceptions such as 'lighter' and 'younger' being the preferred options. That is *not* to say that being short is intrinsically bad: 'petite' conjures up rather a delicate, charming and attractive person, for example.

The point I wish to make is simply that, as teachers, we need to be aware that for some reason, which may be psychological in origin, children tend to have difficulty with the idea of subtraction sums which involve them having items taken away or draws attention to the fact that they are shorter than their colleagues.

Before moving on, the other day a student told me an anecdote which illustrated the point rather well:

> *There were two sweet shops on the way home from school. In the first shop Mr Jones always put a scoop of sweets on the scale and then removed some until he had exactly 250 grams worth. In the second shop Mr Mackay always put half a scoop of sweets on the scale and then added some until he had exactly 250 grams worth. There were always queues in Mr Mackay's shop but never in Mr Jones.*

## Extrinsic home-related problems

In this and the following section the intention is not to apportion blame but rather to examine daily life at home and school and see whether it might — unwittingly — hamper young children's developing understanding of subtraction.

As discussed in the previous chapter, prior to coming to school many children overcome the hazards associated with subtraction when problems are presented in an appropriate context. Thinking about it, I should think that many of the subtraction problems young children solve in their everyday lives, they set themselves: if 4-year-olds Jane and Mary have six and four sweets respectively they will know who has more and probably by how many. They will know which children are younger and older than they are and, assuming the figures are in years and not too high, they can probably work out the difference in ages. Problems may arise, however, when parents and other adults start presenting them with subtraction problems. Take, for example, a Dad who has four sweets and his son, John, who has six. The Dad wants to know how many *more* sweets John has. The problem — as Charles Desforges pointed out to me — is that 'more' may well have been misrepresented to John earlier in his life: when he asked for 'more pudding' he was invariably given less than he started with! Asking him how many more sweets does he have than his Dad therefore may well seem a bizarre question. In other words, John has had an inconsistent experience of certain words.

Another home-related problem is the assumption that eager parents can make following the discovery that their children can recite their numbers. Quite understandably the proud parents want to see their offspring writing and doing 'proper sums'. One thing can lead to another and in no time the parents have bought a book of real sums for their child to work through. Some children have the satisfaction of success but apart from the psychological pressure to perform well there can, for example, be an unfortunate focus on taking away to the detriment of other forms of subtraction. After all, taking away objects tends to be the easiest and most automatic way to demonstrate subtraction. Thus many children may have a limited exposure to subtraction at home.

Another example of a narrow experience occurs when parents show children a set procedure for completing their sums and insist that they should adopt the same method every time. (Some teachers fall into this trap too!) This often makes children less versatile when faced with new problems. The danger of such an approach may not come to light for some time, however, because of another possible limitation in provision: parents — and many teachers too for that matter — tend to present rather standard problems where, typically, the larger figure is presented first and the task is to take away a smaller figure (e.g. $5 - 3 = ?$). It is not until children are faced with problems such as, 'What is the difference between two and six?' that they may encounter difficulties as a result of using any one particular technique.

## Extrinsic school-related problems

As implied above, the potential problems which may arise at home and school are not mutually exclusive. In this section, however, I will focus on situations which are more likely to occur at school than in the home.

Hughes (1986) has demonstrated that young children can frequently solve subtraction problems if they are clearly presented in a practical manner the children can understand. Thinking back to our own school days though, how often were we presented with pages of dry, abstract subtraction sums which, apparently, bore no relationship to anything? I suspect that we — being among the brighter members of society — had little difficulty jumping through the hoops but what about the children who were just learning to form their numbers or who had difficulty relating to the task at hand? Pressure from some parents and the demands of the National Curriculum can mean that in some classrooms this situation is very much still the norm with children being introduced to written work too soon, making it hard for some of them to acquire a real understanding of subtraction. I suspect that for such individuals their frustration and confusion is further increased when, after successfully finishing a page of addition sums, they use the same technique to complete a page of mixed subtraction and addition sums.

In the previous chapter I introduced the idea that care needs to be taken when representing subtraction problems using concrete apparatus. To reduce the likelihood of later difficulties I would suggest that pupils should be given plenty of opportunities to represent subtraction sums using a variety of props. If possible — particularly in the early stages — these should be everyday materials such as pencils, straws and even children so that pupils can identify with the processes. Later, as children gain in confidence and experience, it may be practicable to use more abstract apparatus such as cubes or Dienes blocks, particularly if large numbers are involved. Some older children can be resistant to such aids which can hamper the development of their understanding of subtraction when, for example, decomposition is involved: the skill of the teacher is to remove the stigma of using such equipment.

If a teacher has been brought up to view subtraction simply in terms of 'take away' it is easy to appreciate that he/she might be fairly limited in the range of experiences he/she provides. With confidence and understanding, however, teachers can introduce their pupils to the notion of playing with number bonds (e.g. 'how many ways can you solve 5 + ? = 12?'); of using number lines (although it can be hard if you are right-handed to count backwards from right to left on a horizontal line); of tackling unusually presented sums such as 7 = 4 + ?; of using a range of vocabulary; of braving negative numbers; or, simply, counting backwards from ten. A lack of any one of these experiences can limit a child's understanding of subtraction for, as I suspect is clear, it is a multi-faceted concept which is rather more complex than it might first appear.

## Concluding remarks

In this chapter I have endeavoured to unravel some of the complexities of subtraction. In doing so I hope you have begun to see ways in which some of the potential problems when teaching the subject may be minimised. If, in the past, you have tended to focus on 'taking away' you may be feeling a little overwhelmed or even dispirited. Take heart: most of my students begin their training with a very limited notion of subtraction but, within a couple of sessions, they are very adept at *planning* ways to teach it in a broad and meaningful manner. Actually *teaching* it some of them find a little harder but that is to be expected when their classroom experience as students — let alone teachers — only amounts to a week or so.

## References

HAYLOCK, D. and COCKBURN, A.D. (1997) *Understanding Mathematics in the Lower Primary Years*, London, Paul Chapman Publishing.

HUGHES, M. (1986) *Children and Number*, Oxford, Blackwell.

PIMM, D. (1995) *Symbols and Meanings in School Mathematics*, London, Routledge.

## Chapter 7　　What is time?

At a recent conference of the International Group for the Psychology of Education there were over 240 presentations about all manner of mathematical topics but not one of them mentioned time. Was it because it is such an easy subject there was nothing to say? Or was it because it is such an integral part of life that people have ceased to think about it as a mathematical issue? Whatever the reason, it is clear from my own experience and discussions with teachers that teaching young children to tell the time is far from easy. To our credit I have yet to meet an adult who cannot tell the time: it may be that I live a very sheltered life but I rather suspect that we in the teaching profession — and the demands of everyday life — are by and large successful in teaching time.

In this chapter I will endeavour to discuss some important facets of time and place and our knowledge of it in an historical context. This background should inform our thinking of the problems of teaching time discussed in the next chapter.

## Passing the time

Whitrow (1988) reports that some cultures have few — if any — words which refer to time in their language. Many of us seem to be obsessed by it, particularly when we are under pressure, and yet the Nuer people in Sudan and the Hopi of

FIG 7.1
Time passing

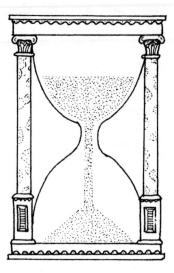

Arizona apparently pay little heed to the notion of time
passing. (What a wonderful idea!) Back to our reality: the
passing of time is a very prominent phenomenon in Western
society which is distinct from, but related to, the telling of
time which will be discussed towards the end of the chapter.

Granted that number, shape and measurement, for example,
are conceptually complex, mathematically they — unlike time
— can be illustrated very easily in practical terms. A child
can count out three bricks and see them. It may take quite
a bit of discussion and practical experience to realise that
three pencils are associated with the same 'threeness' but,
nevertheless, direct comparisons can be made and various
manoeuvres can be carried out to further understanding.
Similarly, although it may be more difficult (see Chapter 9),
shapes can be handled and moved so that the properties of
objects may be compared and contrasted.

Time, on the other hand, is far more elusive. Children
may conduct all manner of experiments seeing how many
jumps they can do in a minute but they can never see or
touch anything that represents the passing of time in a very
satisfactory manner. You may immediately argue that a minute
glass (see Figure 7.1) is a clearly visible representation of time
passing but, even an adult with a well-developed sense of the
passage of time, I defy you to argue that watching a kettle

boil for a minute when you are in a hurry creates the same
impression of time passing as a minute watching a fascinating
film. Moreover, unlike the comparisons between three bricks
and three pencils or between two equilateral triangles, you
cannot generally compare your experiences simultaneously.
You can usually only do it in series: one after the other.
(I suppose you could see how many times you could hop and
say the alphabet in a 3-minute period but I would suggest that
your performance in both would suffer and that it would be
even harder to focus on the passage of time.) So not only is
the passing of time more elusive an experience than counting
but it is also more difficult to compare examples.

## Passing even more time

When teaching the notion of time to young children
we frequently talk about days, weeks, months and years.
Sometimes we refer to the passing of the seasons too. Stopping
to think about it, what concept do you think a child has of a
day or a week, let alone a month or a year? At 6 or 7-years-old
they have hardly had much actual experience of these time
periods and it is debatable as to how much of that could be
termed relevant to the development of their conceptual
understanding of the passage of time.

Taking the argument further, you could ask, where does that
leave the teaching of history? Few of us learn history when we
have actually experienced the passing of decades, let alone
centuries! Perhaps it is not surprising, therefore, that in a study
of several secondary schools, Haydn (1995) found that many
children in Year 7 (11–12 year olds) and above

> ❝ . . . *do not know some of the rudimentary vocabulary and con-
> ventions for measuring time and ordering the past.* (p. 11)

I am not arguing, of course, that young children should not
study history and begin to develop an appreciation of shorter
and longer periods of time; rather I am suggesting that, in the
past, we may have been naive as to the extent of their
understanding.

# Diachronic thinking

Recently I was asked to review a book about diachronic thinking and, I have to confess, I had never heard of the term before! Having reported my ignorance to the reviews editor, I was asked to read the book and see how I got on. This, I am glad to say, I did.

The book, *Understanding Changes in Time: The development of diachronic thinking in 7 to 12 year old children*, is by Jacques Montangero (1996). He acknowledges that the diachronic approach is '. . . little known and largely uncharted territory' (p. 183) and he describes it thus,

> *I consider the diachronic approach to be a perspective which is not content to describe things in time but instead attempts to understand their development and find in the temporal dimension the explanation of current affairs.* (p. 2)

When reading the book I had some reservations about the Piagetian experiments used (Cockburn, forthcoming) but, nonetheless, I think Montangero makes some important observations on children's understanding of the effects of time on, for example, growth and decay in nature. In a series of experiments, children were asked to consider the life cycle of trees in a forest. Montangero concluded,

> *Thus 7 or 8 year old children most certainly know that trees are not eternal . . . Despite this, they do not anticipate the decay or renewal of a forest even in the very long term.* (p. 53)

Taking an example which involved a shorter period of time, Montangero presented children with a series of drawings of Babar and Celeste (story-book characters) on ice which gradually melts. The more pictures he presented between the first and last in the story (i.e. a substantial island of ice to none at all) the longer children thought the drama took to unfold. Furthermore, when the story was extended, the children thought more pictures would be required. For example, when a child of 9.7 years was asked to illustrate what would happen if the ice was put into a cold room, the reply was that the time taken for the story would be, '. . . very long, we will need at least 20 drawings' (p. 63).

So what are we to conclude? I think there are two points I would like to emphasise. The first is that the passing of time seems to be a far more elusive concept to demonstrate at an elementary level than the other mathematical concepts typically taught in the early years of schooling. The second point is that we are only just beginning to understand how children view the effects of the passage of time. Until we know more, this may not have any direct implications for your teaching but, having some appreciation of the fact that a child's thinking may be rather more different from your own than previously thought, may help in the untangling of errors and misconceptions.

## Time measurements

One of the teachers in my mathematics research group asked, 'Why isn't time decimal?' Teaching time would be so much simpler if it were. The thought of decimal time so intrigued me that this section is devoted to a brief history of why we tell the time in the way we do. I am not advocating that the details should become part of the mathematics curriculum but, as with the complexity of counting in the teens (Chapter 3), I think some children might benefit from some insight into the history of time-telling. Knowing, for example, that in the eighth century A.D. the Venerable Bede toyed with the idea of having 22,560 atoms in an hour might make them appreciate how lucky they are!

At the beginning of the chapter I mentioned that some cultures — albeit a minority — appear to have little language pertaining to time. Over the centuries in Europe, however, the need for telling the time arose for a number of practical and scientific reasons. Whitrow (1988) suggests that telling the time was preceded by indicating the passage of time between particular occurrences. Thus, for example, counting the days in terms of dawns — an easily recognisable recurrent phenomenon — is to be found in Homer's writing of sixth century B.C.: 'This is the twelfth dawn since I came to Ilion' (*Iliad*, xxi. 80–81).

Nowadays most of us view the start of our day as when we wake up; technically, however, a day begins at midnight. This was not always the case. Whitrow (1988) reports that Egyptians, for example, chose dawn for the beginning of their day-unit while the Babylonians, Jews and Muslims opted for sunset. Astronomers, such as Ptolemy (second century A.D.), found midday a more convenient starting point for their calculations and it was not until 1st January 1925 that an international agreement was reached that decreed that the 'day' started at midnight.

Clearly such conventions are important in times of a shrinking world and greater communications but such uniformity seemed irrelevant in Babylonian times. They divided daylight time equally into twelve 'hours' but, not only did the length of these hours vary according to the time of year, they also varied according to where you were (Dohrn van Rossum, 1996). Thus, for example, the shortest 'hour' experienced in the winter in Upper Egypt was equivalent to fifty-three of our modern minutes whereas in Northern England in the winter an 'hour' could be as short as thirty minutes. In the height of summer the Egyptian hour was considerably shorter than the English hour being sixty-seven minutes as opposed to ninety.

These temporal hours — 'horae temporals' — were also used by our forebears in fourteenth-century Britain and, according to Whitrow (1972), there were 'usually twelve'. Ten of these were the interval from sunrise to sunset with an additional two for morning and evening twilight respectively. Thus, again, there was variation in the length of an hour according to the time of year: although, interestingly, Whitrow goes on to say that astronomers used hours of a standard length — 'horae equinoctials' — and these were the equivalent to a temporal hour at the date of the spring equinox. Moreover, hundreds of years previously, Greek astronomers had divided each equinoctial hour into sixty minute units. These units were further divided into sixty seconds (Whitrow, 1988).

We cannot hold the Greeks entirely responsible for the lack of decimalisation, however, for they were following earlier Babylonian conventions which used a base of sixty — rather than ten — for their place value system. In actual fact the

Babylonians did have a symbol for ten (i.e. a broad sideways wedge somewhat similar to ◄ ) but their only other symbol was for a unit (a thin vertical wedge akin to ▾) making fifty-nine rather cumbersome

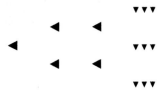

Hughes (1986) explains that, to make sixty, the Babylonians struck upon the idea that the same symbol could represent different numbers if one varied its position in relation to the other symbols. Thus, if the symbol for one is written to the left of ten symbols, it represents sixty. Eighty-one, for example, was written as

A final concept which was important to our forebears was that of a year. It became important in agricultural areas where seasonal variations were significant. To a certain extent climatic changes could be used to determine the start and end of the year but, as they required greater accuracy for sowing, primitive man learnt to appreciate that the rising and setting of the stars formed the basis of a calendar year (Whitrow, 1988).

Such 'heliacal' risings and settings however did not help in dividing the year up into units which were longer than days but shorter than a year. Originally the waxing and waning of the moon was used but, as it did not coincide with the solar period (i.e. the time it takes for the earth to revolve round the sun), the system was abandoned and our months are now an arbitrary way of dividing the solar year into twelve parts (Whitrow, 1988).

Interestingly it was not until 1752 that the United Kingdom adapted the same calendar as that used in most Western European countries. It was accompanied by considerable furore and cries of 'Give us back our eleven days' when the Government decreed that the day following 2nd September should be 14th September and the workers worried about their wages.

## Concluding remarks

In the past — and even in a few cultures today — time was (is) of little relevance to the vast majority of people. As needs arose, ways of considering the passage of time emerged. Often these were idiosyncratic and depended on the time of year and the lifestyle of the people concerned. Methods of measuring time in more systematic ways came about with the introduction of devices such as sundials in the third millenium B.C. (Dohrn van Rossum, 1996) and a wide variety of mechanical instruments among the earliest of which was apparently to be seen in the Palace of the Visconti in Milan in 1335 (Whitrow, 1988). Nowadays many of us feel beseiged by time, being surrounded by a never-ending barrage of demands and constant reminders of what time it is. Interestingly, however, as will be discussed in the next chapter, an understanding of time is not easily acquired . . .

## References

COCKBURN, A.D. (forthcoming) 'Review of Montangero's book', *The British Journal of Educational Psychology.*

DOHRN VAN ROSSUM, G.D. (1996) *History of the Hour,* Chicago, The University of Chicago Press.

HAYDN, T. (1995) 'Teaching children about time', *Teaching History,* **81**, pp. 11–12.

HUGHES, M. (1986) *Children and Number,* Oxford, Blackwell.

MONTANGERO, J. (1996) *Understanding Changes in Time,* London, Taylor and Francis.

WHITROW, G.J. (1972) *What is Time?* London, Thames and Hudson.

WHITROW, G.J. (1988) *Time in History,* Oxford, Oxford University Press.

## Chapter 8    The problems of teaching time

In the last chapter I described various attributes of time
which I hope will have given you more of an insight into the
complexities of the subject. Keeping these thoughts in mind, I
suggest you have a go at brainstorming the potential problems
you might encounter when teaching time. To help you, you
might also cast your mind back to the suggestions made at the
beginning of Chapter 6, i.e. think about:

- the different forms of time described in the previous
  chapter and any related difficulties;
- your own experiences of learning the subject;
- any problems you have encountered when teaching time in
  the past;
- observations of, and conversations with, pupils at work and
  the type of errors they make, recalling, if possible, any
  insight you might have into such errors;
- discussion you might have had with colleagues and other
  adults;
- anything you might have read about time.

Next, I suggest you categorise the potential problems in a
way that is helpful to you. Below, I will remind you of the
categories I used when considering subtraction but, when I
tried to apply these myself to potential problems with time,
I ended up with a rather cramped diagram with arrows going
everywhere! Accordingly I decided to focus on the two main
concepts of time separately. Thus its *passage* and the *telling* of
it — as discussed in the last chapter — result in two diagrams

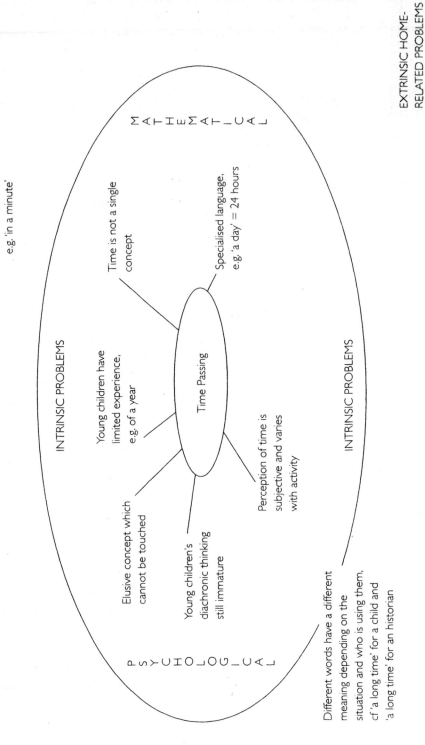

EXTRINSIC SCHOOL-
RELATED PROBLEMS

EXTRINSIC HOME-
RELATED PROBLEMS

Imprecise use of time-related words,
e.g. 'in a minute'

INTRINSIC PROBLEMS

Time is not a single
concept

Specialised language,
e.g. 'a day' = 24 hours

Young children have
limited experience,
e.g. of a year

Time Passing

Perception of time is
subjective and varies
with activity

INTRINSIC PROBLEMS

Elusive concept which
cannot be touched

Young children's
diachronic thinking
still immature

Different words have a different
meaning depending on the
situation and who is using them,
cf 'a long time' for a child and
'a long time' for an historian

MATHEMATICAL

PSYCHOLOGICAL

FIG 8.1
Some potential problems when teaching the passage of time

with the problems related to each presented in turn. In that way, when considering the teaching of a particular aspect of time, I can be more focused in my thoughts rather than facing a mass of potential problems, some of which may not be relevant. (I also end up with two fairly tidy diagrams rather than one messy one.) If you remember, in Chapter 6, I found the following categories helpful but you may come up with others more suited to you.

1  Intrinsic mathematical problems (imp)
2  Intrinsic psychological problems (ipp)
3  Extrinsic home-related problems (ehp)
4  Extrinsic school-related problems (esp)

Again I should stress that the list of potential problems is not exhaustive.

## Problems with the passage of time

The temptation here is to put 'numerous', sigh and leave it at that. Most of us in the Western world seemed to be obsessed with the passing of time and, as an extract from Haylock and Cockburn (1997) demonstrates, in the English language we have a multitude of words relating to time:

❝ *how long, second, minute, hour, day, week, fortnight, month, quarter, year, leap year, decade, century, millennium, season, spring, summer, autumn, winter, week-end, term, life-time, long time, short time, brief, temporary, for the time being, long-lasting, interval, pause, cycle, period, extra time, non-stop, never-ending, permanent, on and on, how old, age, age-group, year-group, teenager, young, old, elderly, middle-aged, under-age, ancient, modern, up-to-date, older, elder, oldest, younger, youngest, when, daytime, night-time, dawn, sunrise, morning, tea-time, break-time, lunch-time (etc.), noon, midday, after-noon, dusk, sunset, evening, midnight, small hours, matinee, past, present, future, spell, then, now, before, after, next, previous, earlier, prior, following, later, afterwards, due, eventually, in the long run, in due course, never, always, once, once upon a time, one day, recent, soon, immediately, straightaway, in a moment, instantly, in a jiffy, while, meanwhile, till, until, up to, not yet, in the meantime, during, nowadays, sometime, sooner or later, at the last minute, often, frequent, daily, hourly, weekly, monthly, annually, occasionally, regularly, now and again, every so often, from time to time, sometimes, hardly ever, once in a blue moon, clock, watch, sundial, timer, egg-timer, meter, tick, tick-tock, dial, face, alarm, setting, hands, minute-hand, hour-hand, digits, (e.g.) three twenty-five, o'clock, a.m., half past, quarter to, quarter past, five past (etc.), twenty-five to (etc.), 24 hour clock, fourteen hours (etc.), timetable, zero hour, summer time, put clocks forward and back, overtime, half-time, slow, fast, on time, late, early, punctual, diary, calendar, date, Sunday, Monday, Tuesday, etc., yesterday, today, tomorrow, last week, January, February, etc., first, second, third, etc., nineteenth century, twentieth century, twenty-first century (etc.), birthday, anniversary, mark time, beat time, keep time, rhythm, short notice, advance notice, afterthought, postpone, put off, waste time, . . .* (pp. 103–4)

Despite so many words and phrases to choose from, however, we are frequently very imprecise when talking to children — 'In a minute we'll do x' — so perhaps it is no wonder that they have little concept of how long it takes for a minute to pass. Related to this problem is the fact that the passing of time is an elusive concept in so far as it cannot be touched and can only be 'seen' through an intermediate means such as a minute glass or a second-hand spinning round.

Added to which one's personal perception of the passage of time is subjective and dependent on what you are doing: what seems like an hour to you in the dentist's chair may seem like five minutes to the dentist and may, in reality, be twenty minutes. (Having said that the reality is likely to be even nearer the dentist's perception as professionals who work to a strict time schedule generally develop a fairly clear idea as to how long an appointment is lasting.)

Taking this a step further, the issue is complicated when one considers time from an historical perspective. As I mentioned in the last chapter, young children have very limited experience of a year: the time between one birthday and the next seems an inordinately long time! It is perhaps not so surprising, therefore, when they ask you or their parents questions such as 'What was it like for you when there were no cars/electricity/glass for windows?'

Related to the above is the idea of being able to sequence events in a logical order. This is a common exercise in many primary schools and is generally seen both as a mathematical activity and a preparation for telling stories. Problems may arise, however, if one fails to appreciate a child's perspective or poses the task in an inappropriate manner. For example, from a logical perspective, if one is asked at 11am, 'which comes first lunch or breakfast?' one could be right in replying 'lunch'. That, unfortunately, is not usually the 'correct' answer. As it happens most children seem to latch on to what their teachers want when asked such questions but I think it could be made more straightforward if such requests were preceded by a preface such as 'Imagine you are waking up in the morning . . .' or rephrased thus, 'Think about what you have done so far today, which meal comes next?'

As described in the previous chapter, diachronic thinking is, in a sense, an extension of the ordering process as it is an appreciation of how the passage of time can affect situations involving change such as growth and decay. Observing cress, sunflowers or all manner of things growing can act as an introduction. In many reception classes you see pictures of the children when they were babies and as they are now. There are several reasons as to why this is a worthwhile activity but, as 5-year-olds will have no recollection of being a baby, I am not sure that it is a task to aid diachronic thinking. Something faster and visual — such as cooking — seems more appropriate.

## Telling the time

As I said in the previous chapter: adults appear to be able to tell the time with no difficulty. If you stop to think about it, however, we seem to have made telling the time inordinately difficult.

To start with we have a vast number of ways in which to refer to a particular time. Off the top of my head there is, 'twenty-five to ten'

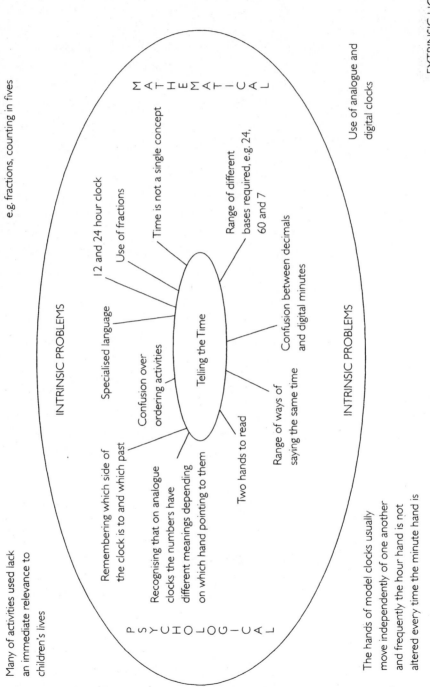

EXTRINSIC SCHOOL-
RELATED PROBLEMS

Many of activities used lack
an immediate relevance to
children's lives

Lack of necessary prerequisite skills,
e.g. fractions, counting in fives

EXTRINSIC HOME-
RELATED PROBLEMS

INTRINSIC PROBLEMS

INTRINSIC PROBLEMS

MATHEMATICAL

PSYCHOLOGICAL

Telling the Time

12 and 24 hour clock

Use of fractions

Time is not a single concept

Range of different
bases required, e.g. 24,
60 and 7

Specialised language

Confusion over
ordering activities

Confusion between decimals
and digital minutes

Remembering which side of
the clock is to and which past

Recognising that on analogue
clocks the numbers have
different meanings depending
on which hand pointing to them

Two hands to read

Range of ways of
saying the same time

Use of analogue and
digital clocks

The hands of model clocks usually
move independently of one another
and frequently the hour hand is not
altered every time the minute hand is

FIG 8.2
**Some potential problems when teaching the telling of time**

or 'nine thirty-five'
or, more precisely, 'twenty-five to ten in the evening'
or 'nine thirty-five in the evening'
or, more succinctly, 'nine thirty-five pm'
or, more continentally, 'twenty-one thirty-five'.

Over the last twenty years, digital clocks seem to have taken off — they are on videos, microwaves, cookers, wrists — but, even allowing for our conservative nature, analogue clocks are still here — on Big Ben, in cars, on wrists — and it looks like we will be teaching time using both methods for some time to come.

There are several advantages to the analogue clock when learning to tell the time because, although it may be difficult (see below), it is generally there for you to see: the hours are written in one to twelve, the minutes are shown and, when you get on to halves and quarters, the clock face can be divided up quite easily.

One problem which can arise when using analogue clocks, however, is that we underestimate the difficulty of focusing on two hands simultaneously. Not only that, but we can exacerbate the problem by only moving one of the hands when we alter the time on a model clock. For example we may switch from discussing four o'clock to focusing on half past four but only move the minute hand in the process. To avoid this problem I would recommend introducing young children to clock faces which only have one hand: the hour hand. In that way the initial focus would be on the hours which are all clearly marked with appropriate numbers round the clock. This would be accompanied by much realistic discussion about everyday activities which actually do happen on the hour. It may take a bit of reorganisation but, as Figure 8.2 suggests, another potential problem is making time telling artificial and irrelevant.

The next step would be to point the hour hand somewhere between, for example, the three and the four on the clock face and encourage the children to tell you whether they think the hand is just *past* the three, near *to* the four or half-way between. Again this could be related to everyday activities such as, 'we go home at just a little bit *past* three' or 'we go outside when the hand is nearly pointing *to* the eleven'. Such activities are likely to take the burden off children having to remember which side of the clock face is 'to' and which 'past'.

One handed clocks are of limited value unless they are big enough for you to make accurate estimates of the minutes between the hours but, once children are secure with one hand, they can be introduced to the other. This can be tricky because the introduction of minutes brings, in effect, the super imposition of one scale upon another: the '1' on the clock face no longer just means 'one o'clock' but it *also* represents five minutes past the hour; the '2' means 'two o'clock' *and* ten past and so on. Perhaps this is a good time to introduce the five times table! It might also be a good time to explain a little about how we come to tell the time in the way we do. I am not necessarily suggesting that you go into the detail of the previous chapter but rather that you perhaps make a point of sharing with children some of the seemingly quirky conventions of time telling.

The idea of half past should be relatively straightforward having encouraged the children to look at the hour hand (which will be in the correct position rather than left pointing at the hour as might have happened in some classrooms in the past.) Although I am rather against the artificiality of paper clocks, this might also be the time to fold the 'clock' in half and, in due course, quarters to help with the potential problems which might arise from a lack of practical, realistic experience with fractions.

It is perhaps of interest to note that, without consciously thinking about it, I opted to discuss analogue clocks before digital; is it my age or is it a simpler way to start teaching the time? I suspect it is a combination of both but, as shown in Figure 8.2, there are potential problems with both.

Learning that there are twenty-four hours in a day probably comes best when your focus is on digital clocks. This is yet another example of precise specialist language in mathematics: until they are specifically taught otherwise, most children will consider 'a day' to refer to daylight rather than the twenty-four hours shown on the clock.

Personally I do not think you can 'see' the passing of time so well on a digital clock although, while recognising that I might be biased, I do concede that you can watch the minutes changing.

In some ways, telling the time from a digital clock is considerably easier than using an analogue as there is only one dial and you can more or less just read the numbers off if you know the convention of reading the first two figures as a numeral and then the second two (remembering to omit the zero if the first number is, for example, '05'). Some clocks would automatically omit the zero in which case the child needs to appreciate that the two digits after the dots are always read as one numeral.

Using the twenty-four hour clock is a perfectly common way of telling the time if one is travelling but it is still fairly unusual to talk about '*seventeen* fifty-five', for example, in everyday conversation. This problem is avoided on digital clocks with 'am' and 'pm' but, without these, some discussion of the twenty-four hour clock and common usage is warranted. Fortunately the 'fifty-five' of 'seventeen fifty-five' is now perfectly acceptable and so, for the time being, children are able to avoid the potential problems of 'past' and 'to' when telling the time.

Nor do they have to confront the issue of fractions as 'five fifteen', 'five thirty' and 'five forty-five' are all part of common usage. Problems may arise, however, if, rather than a child telling the time, he or she has to interpret someone else's reading of it: 'what on earth is quarter past five?'

A final, potentially significant, problem with digital clocks is the possible confusion with decimals. The convention on clocks is to have two dots in mid-air separating the hours and the minutes, e.g. 5 : 34. The convention when writing decimals is obviously different (e.g. 5 . 34) but, nonetheless, to a novice in a hurry reading the time out of context there may be difficulties. As in other similar situations, I suggest you make the conventions explicit to minimise the possibility of confusion.

## Concluding remarks

Teaching children to tell the time and have an appreciation of the passage of time is not something that can be done overnight. As with any topic it is important to be clear about your aims at any particular time, recognise the potential complexities and act accordingly. This need not involve detailed explanations but rather the building up of ideas in a relevant and practical manner.

You may have noticed that I have opted out of any mention of seconds or adding or subtracting time. They all bring their own complications largely to do with the range of bases we use when working with time: *sixty* seconds in a minute, *sixty* minutes in an hour but *twenty-four* hours in a day and *seven* days in a week and so on. Fortunately, in the early years of schooling, we only need to introduce the bases not convert between them.

## Reference

HAYLOCK, D. and COCKBURN, A. (1997) *Understanding Mathematics in the Lower Primary Years,* London, Paul Chapman Publishing.

## Chapter 9    Thinking about shape

The idea for a chapter on shape came from my primary teachers' mathematics research group. I was happy to go along with the suggestion as they seemed keen and I thought it would add an interesting and important contrast to the chapters on numeracy and time. Having said that, I was well aware that my experience of researching shape, let alone teaching it at any level, was limited. Unfortunately, as luck would have it, the 'shape and space' session was cancelled and I was left rather more to my own devices than originally intended. I had two options: to forget all about it and consider the possibility of writing on a topic I knew more about, or to persevere. As you can see, I chose the second option. There were a wide variety of reasons for doing so, but most relevantly:

- I thought if I was expecting, among others, novice teachers to adopt the approach outlined in this book then I ought to find out whether — with my limited experience of shape — I could do the same.
- I have found that one of the best ways to learn about something is to have to use it for a purpose such as teaching, writing or — if the 'something' is, for example, carpentry — mending a chair. (As an educationalist I often encourage my students to give their pupils meaningful activities to encourage purposeful learning: here is a case of my endeavouring to practice what I preach.)
- When reading about the subject it soon becomes clear that,

*. . . spatial thinking, which obviously undergirds geometry, has been suggested by famous mathematicians such as Hadamard and Einstein to be essential to creative thought in all high level mathematics. Given their importance, therefore, it is essential that geometry and spatial reasoning receive greater attention in instruction and in research.*

(Clements and Battista, 1992, p. 457)

At a less esoteric level Ben-Chaim et al. (1989) point out that graphical representations of three-dimensional shapes,

*. . . are commonly used in a great number of practical situations and disciplines for conveying spatial information, for example maps, diagrams, flow-charts, and scientific or technical descriptive drawings . . . Providing all pupils with opportunity to explore a variety of types of representations of spatial and geometric information, as well as to communicate such representations should be a basic educational objective.* (p. 121)

Clements and Battista (1992) have expressed concern that young children in the United States are not receiving a sufficient grounding in basic geometric concepts and cite Stigler et al.'s work (cited in Clements and Battista, 1992) that shows that their performance on visualisation and paper-folding tests is far poorer than that of their Japanese counterparts. I have not found comparative studies of pupils in the United Kingdom but, with a growing emphasis on numeracy and a tendency to teach shape in whole class sessions, I suspect we have little room for complacency.

I would suggest that early years work on shape is, conceptually, relatively straightforward. Therefore, rather than launching into a mathematical explanation of the topic — which, in any event, others can do better than I can (see, for example, Haylock, 1995; Dickson et al., 1984; Williams and Shuard, 1994) — I will move on to a consideration of the potential problems without further ado.

## Brainstorming

As with previous topics, I suggest you begin by brainstorming the potential problems associated with the teaching of shape to young children. Then, if you find it helpful, categorise them into what the source of the problem might be (e.g. intrinsically mathematical or psychological or extrinsically home- or school-related). As will be apparent below, these categorisations are not always mutually exclusive when it comes to shape but, nonetheless, I think they have value in helping to find proactive strategies which can reduce the number of potential problems.

I suspect the results of your brainstorming might, to a certain extent, be different from mine but I hope the two will complement each other and that each will provide additional insight (see Figure 9.1).

## Intrinsic mathematical problems

Geometric shapes are, by their very nature, abstract,

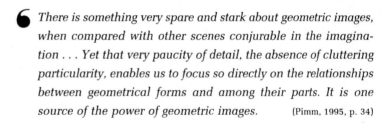

> There is something very spare and stark about geometric images, when compared with other scenes conjurable in the imagination . . . Yet that very paucity of detail, the absence of cluttering particularity, enables us to focus so directly on the relationships between geometrical forms and among their parts. It is one source of the power of geometric images.   (Pimm, 1995, p. 34)

A related, but not solely mathematical, problem is that two and three dimensional shapes look different depending on the angle from which they are viewed. You could argue that the same is true of chairs and yet children have little difficulty in repeatedly recognising them.

As with the other topics discussed in this book, learning about shape involves the appreciation of the distinction between specialised language and that of everyday. 'Faces' on a cube, for example, are likely to be a challenge to start with for, not only are there more than one, but some are the same and

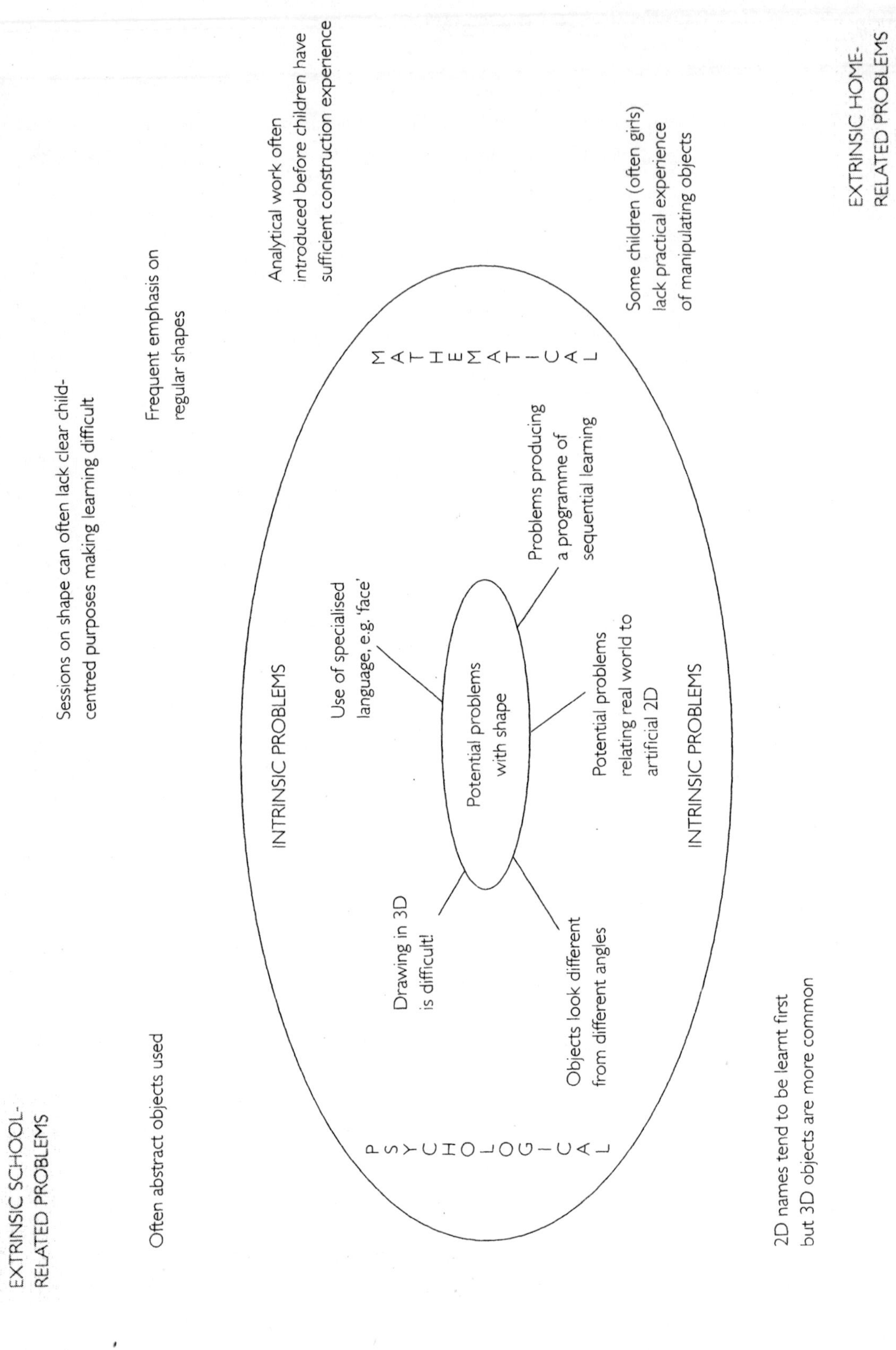

EXTRINSIC SCHOOL-
RELATED PROBLEMS

Sessions on shape can often lack clear child-
centred purposes making learning difficult

Frequent emphasis on
regular shapes

Analytical work often
introduced before children have
sufficient construction experience

EXTRINSIC HOME-
RELATED PROBLEMS

Some children (often girls)
lack practical experience
of manipulating objects

Often abstract objects used

MATHEMATICAL

Problems producing
a programme of
sequential learning

INTRINSIC PROBLEMS

Use of specialised
language, e.g. 'face'

Potential problems
with shape

Potential problems
relating real world to
artificial 2D

INTRINSIC PROBLEMS

Drawing in 3D
is difficult!

Objects look different
from different angles

PSYCHOLOGICAL

2D names tend to be learnt first
but 3D objects are more common

FIG 9.1
**Potential problems with shape**

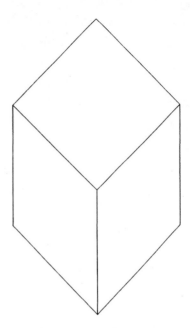

others are different. And what about Figure 9.2: a corner is 'facing' us!

Clements and Battista (1992) argue that attention needs to be drawn to the differences between the common and mathematical usage of words, pointing out,

 *... when mathematical language is used too early and when the teacher does not use everyday speech as a point of reference, mathematical language is learned without concomitant mathematical understanding.* (p. 433)

The naming of the actual shapes also needs to be done with care. Pimm (1995) cites Richard Feynman's anecdote about his father telling him,

 *You can know the name of that bird in all the languages of the world, but when you're finished, you'll know absolutely nothing about the bird. You'll only know about humans in different places and what they call the bird, so let's look at the bird and see what it's* doing — *that's what counts.*

(Pimm, 1995, p. xiii, from Feynman, 1988, p. 14)

When I first read this I agreed, only to find that Pimm thought that it was 'fundamentally wrong'. He argues that naming is done for a reason and that a name can convey much information. What about your names, for example, where do they come from? Johnson, Davidson and Richardson were, at one time, the sons of John, David and Richard. Pimm (1995) points out that, not only does naming allow you to talk about things it,

> ❝ . . . also allows classification — and the use of the same name (or root, e.g. 'hexa', 'bi') invites pupils to look for similarities between things. However, naming per se is not the point of the exercise. In its worst form the purposes behind geometrical naming get lost and the process degenerates into a sort of feeble natural history of shapes.
>
> ( p. xiii, brackets added)

The final potential problem in this section is, in a sense, mathematical but it is also psychological and related to the way shape is taught in school. The two questions we need to consider here are: Is the learning of shape a hierarchical process? Should shape be taught in whole class sessions? The brief answers are: the jury is still out, and probably not but it often is (i.e. taught in whole class situations).

There has been considerable research on the first question — Is the learning of shape a hierarchical process? — and both Piaget and Van Hiele have contributed much to the process in the last forty years (see, for example, Clements and Battista, 1992). Both produced models of geometric thinking which have much to commend them. It is, however, still unclear as to how accurate they are and whether the levels they propose are discrete stages through which individuals move in a systematic order.

Rather than describe the models in detail, therefore, I think we should turn to the second question — Should shape be taught in whole class sessions? — as, at the moment, this has more immediate and practical relevance. My view is that it should not be in a formal sense although, from time to time, aspects of geometry may be mentioned to the whole class in passing. My argument is based on the range of potential problems discussed in this chapter and, in particular, the fact that children come to the subject with a wide variety of experiences and understandings. This is encapsulated in an extract from some work I did with Charles Desforges,

> *Mrs. G. set out to introduce her third year infants to the names of three dimensional shapes. She had the children sitting in a circle on the carpet. They had established that a globe was sphere shaped. A globe had been passed round. Its spherical properties had been pointed out and felt.*
>
> *Mrs. G.:  Sphere. That's right. Now can anyone else tell me any-*
> *           thing that's a sphere? Adam? (who has his hand up)*
> *Adam:  Square.*
>
> *At this point Mrs. G. recalled, 'I was ever so surprised he said that. I nearly fell off the chair. He is so keen and so shy. I thought 'how on earth am I going to cope with this without putting him down, without smashing the bit of confidence he has got? It really was about the most inappropriate thing he could have said.'*
>
> *She decided to ignore his answer and to get Adam to feel the globe and describe it as a sphere. She then turned her attention to another child. Seconds later, in giving a further example of an everyday object that is a sphere, Ben offered 'Half the world.' Mrs. G. noted*
>
> *'I thought, oh dear! I cannot get into all that now. If he had said it later when we had got the main idea established I could have developed it using plasticene. As it was, lots of the children were just beginning to get the idea and I thought it would be too confusing. I suspect he (Ben) had the idea and would have benefited from some extension but I decided to pass over his suggestion for the sake of the rest of them.'*
>
> *There followed a ten second period of acceptable responses for sphere shaped objects and then Samantha suggested, 'a circle'. Mrs. G. thought,*
>
> *'Help! This is going to be a lot more difficult than I thought. How am I going to explain the difference between a circle and a sphere?'*

*In an attempt to do this she asked Samantha to put her hands all around the globe and then asked her to compare that with a circle (a hula hoop on the floor). As the child did so it occurred to Mrs. G. that Samantha would be able to feel the depth of the hoop and she thought,*

*'We were getting deeper and deeper into it. What could I use? I haven't got the time to cut a circle out of paper. I'll have to make do with the hula hoop and hope she sees the difference. If I cut out a circle the point might be lost and the group might lose interest.'*                    (Desforges and Cockburn, 1987, pp. 113–14)

I have no reason to think that the range of thinking in Mrs G's class was any wider than in any other class: in other words, teaching shapes to a class is exceedingly difficult if not impossible in my view.

The recognition of abstract shapes of course exacerbates the situation. This will be considered in more detail below but, the point I want to make here is that, in the relative absence of distinguishing features, shapes can be difficult to classify if seen from an unusual angle: chairs generally have four legs, a base, a back and arms too if you are lucky but a cylinder just seems to have roundness and length.

In passing, Pimm (1995) makes an interesting point that straight and circular forms rarely occur in nature and then only imperfectly although we might 'see' them in a tree trunk or a full moon respectively. He adds, however, that geometrical drawings have been in existence for at least as long as written records.

## Intrinsic psychological problems

Despite the starkness of geometric shapes, Gray said in his lecture at the 1997 Psychology of Mathematics Education Conference,

*In any situation involving objects the individual has the option of focusing on different aspects of the situation.*

FIG 9.3
Gal and Vinner's task

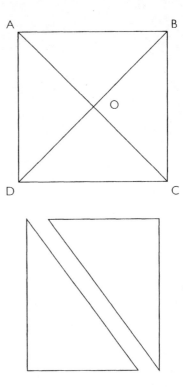

FIG 9.4
Possible perception of a square

This has been clearly illustrated by Gal and Vinner (1997) in their work with ninth grade slow learners in Israel. (I appreciate that the children were older than the focus of this book and the task a little more complex than the other examples here but, bear with me, as I think the point is an important one.) The children were presented with the following square with diagonals AC and DB (see Figure 9.3).

Their task was to check if the diagonals of the square were perpendicular to one another. Previously it had been established that the children knew the meaning of the terms 'diagonal' and 'perpendicular' but, despite this, when faced with the above they could not 'see' — even with encouragement and persuasion — the right angles in question. Initially the children said that ABC and ADC were right angles making the researchers wonder whether, in effect, they saw the figure as two triangles as shown in Figure 9.4.

If this were the case, it is not surprising that the children were unable to identify the required angles as they are not included in the sub-figures seen in Figure 9.4.

One of the conversations with a teacher and pupil in the study went further as, after a while, the child suddenly realised that BAD and BCD were also right angles. The discussion concluded thus,

> **Teacher:** *When I speak about diagonals which are perpendicular to one another, their point of intersection has 90°. Where is that point?*
>
> S:  *(points to 0)*
>
> T:  *Now tell me if an angle of 90° is formed between this diagonal (points to AC) and this diagonal (points to BD)*
>
> S:  *(points to angle ABC!)*        (Gal and Vinner, 1997, p. 286)

Now it could be that the children really did not understand what was being asked of them but, having seen videotapes of the classroom interactions during the course of the study, I would be surprised if it were the case. I am not denying that it is a possibility but a look at Figure 9.5 may further make the point of how it can be difficult to change our focus.

Anderson's 'good continuity principle' suggests that most people will see line WZ and curve XY rather than WY or XZ (Gal and Vinner, 1997).

In brief, we may make assumptions that the focus of other people's attention is very similar to our own when, in fact, how they perceive a figure — or even divide it into sub-figures — may be rather different.

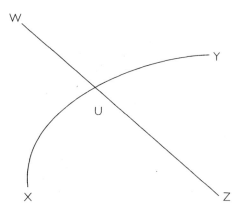

FIG 9.5
Anderson's 'good continuity
principle'

## Teaching shape

To the uninitiated I suspect the teaching of shape seems quite straightforward: produce a box of shapes and teach the children the names and properties of said shapes. Alas, to do the job properly it is not that simple. In this section I will endeavour to explain why this is the case.

Research suggests, not surprisingly, that it is important that children have plenty of practical experiences of looking at pictures and handling shapes early on in their geometry education (Clements and Battista, 1992). Gathering the information on the subject, however, reveals five major considerations as outlined below.

### Representation

The representation of two-dimensional objects is a real problem, as Pimm (1995) points out:

> ❝ *We can imagine a circle with no thickness that is perfectly round, but we can never create one by drawing freehand or even with a pair of compasses. Using the computer language logo to get the turtle to draw a circle . . . brings us up against the difference between an image on a screen and a 'real' circle. But the development of our geometric perception also allows us to see these traces, as circles.*  (p. 33)

Pimm goes on to say that, 'seeing *as* is a very important part of geometry — it allows us to "read" objects and images in a geometrical way' (p. 33).

Davis (1997) gave a clear example of how quickly children adapt to the idea of 'seeing *as*' when, on being required to draw a rectangle, a child produced a figure very similar to that in Figure 9.6.

The following conversation then followed:

> ❝ *T: Can you tell be about these (pointing to the corners)*
> *C: These are supposed to be square (pointing to the corners)*
> *T: (pointing to the dots) What are these?*
> *C: They're not there.*

**FIG 9.6**
'A rectangle'

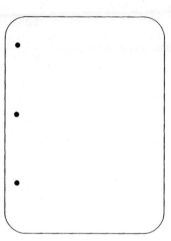

Sometimes adaptability can go even further. Gemma, for example, had just been learning about cubes when I showed her a picture of a square and had the following chat with her:

> *AC: What shape is this?*
> *G:   It's a square . . . (long pause) . . . No, it's a cube. We call it*
>      *a cube in school.*

I suspect Gemma was basing her answer on what she had just been focusing on at school rather than following her instincts. Nevertheless, it raises the issue of two-dimensional representation of three-dimensional objects.

## Active learning

From an early age young children are encouraged to build objects out of various items of junk to develop their appreciation of shapes and their properties. There is nothing whatever wrong with this activity in and of itself but teachers must not be misled into thinking that their pupils are necessarily gaining mathematical insight:

> *A common current belief seems to be that mathematical con-*
> *cepts can be more easily grasped if they are 'represented by' or*
> *'embodied in' physical objects. Need a teacher only provide the*
> *right apparatus for mathematics to be present? Is mathematics*
> *somehow in the equipment? If so, handling it alone may be*
> *sufficient to allow for learning to occur, by osmosis perhaps.*
>
> (Pimm, 1995, p. 13)

Pimm further argues that even if a teacher sets up a situation as a potential mathematical experience, the aim of the exercise may be diluted or even lost on the pupils as they are too busy focusing on the activity itself rather than the mathematics within it. Presenting appropriate tasks and encouraging pupils to see whether the mathematics is in an activity is obviously, therefore, a central part of a teacher's role. Pimm (1995) suggests paper-folding activities which do just that. For example, a child might be asked to fold a piece of paper twice, cut off a corner, sit on the folded paper and then be challenged by the teacher to predict what the shape will be when the paper is unfolded. You may wonder — as I did — why the child was encouraged to sit on the paper. I thought it was to add interest but Pimm argues that it is just one of several devices to interrupt the physical immediacy of the situation and thus encourage a time for reflection and prediction.

## Encouraging language

It is all very well for me to say that teachers should encourage pupils' use of language but I appreciate that it is not always as easy as it sounds with a large class of noisy children.

Logo's turtle graphics are a very good way of fostering pupils' language of shape and space. Pimm (1995) points out, however, that the 'REPEAT' button can sabotage your good intentions for, by pressing it alone, children can come up with some very spectacular results. Having said that, you can always ask the child how they achieved the effects or, better still, challenge them to find another way to produce a similar pattern.

Getting children to work in pairs can also promote their use of language. For example, one child draws a picture — or you give them one — and, hiding it from the other child, he/she has to describe it using words such as 'straight', circle, square so that his/her partner can reproduce the original.

'Haptic' exploration is also to be encouraged. While you may not use this particular term you are probably familiar with 'feely' bags and the 'haptic' explanation they encourage when children take it in turns to select a shape from the bag and

Triadafillidis (1995) conducted a study on 203 Greek, 313 Scottish and 64 American teenagers to determine whether haptic experience helped children later identify objects visually presented on a worksheet. Although she recognises that data from one study is insufficient to prove that haptic exploration can 'promote the learning of geometric shapes or the remediation of misunderstandings', her results do support the notion that cross-modal communication may well be a valuable educational tool. In other words, in this case, handling objects without seeing them appeared to help pupils in their later visual identification of them.

Interestingly she noted that the Greek pupils were better than their English-speaking counterparts at naming various geometric shapes. She thinks this may be because many shape names are Greek in origin. Fortunately, over time, I have noted that children do gain an understanding of prefixes such as 'bi', 'tri', 'hexa' and so on.

describe its properties in order to guess what shape it is without looking at it. Not only does this develop language but it also demands that the children actively focus on geometrical concepts.

## Orientation

If you flick through a mathematics textbook you are likely to see lots of equilateral triangles and lots of squares with their edges parallel to the sides of the page but probably none even slightly tilted. The result of such standard reproductions of shapes is that some children fail to recognise other, less regular, examples of triangles or do not appreciate that a diamond is a square at an angle. The good news is that there is no such problem with circles but this, I am afraid, is the only shape which is straightforward in this respect.

## Properties

Earlier in the chapter I touched upon the potential confusion of representing three-dimensional shapes in a two-dimensional manner such as in a worksheet. From an early age some young children have experience of many objects being represented two dimensionally in their picture books and they appear to have no difficulty in recognising them. Other children are not so privileged: does this affect their ability to 'read' pictures I wonder? How do such representations affect all children's ability to appreciate that cylinders roll whereas cubes are generally highly reluctant to do so?

In part the problem as it relates to three-dimensional shapes can fairly easily be solved by presenting children with objects and giving them tasks — which may be as simple as sorting — to ascertain their properties.

This is not so easy with two dimensional shapes which, for a start, as discussed above, cannot be represented in a very accurate manner: circles do not have 'thickness' although poleidoblocs — which are often used to represent them — do. Geoboards (see Figure 9.7) can be a useful tool for representing a range of two-dimensional shapes quickly and accurately. For example, using one pin as a common point, different coloured elastic bands can be used to illustrate a wide variety of

FIG 9.7
An example of a geoboard

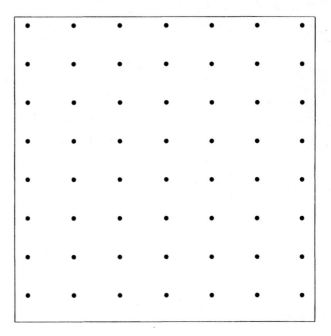

triangles of varying shapes and sizes but all exhibiting the same properties of three sidedness and angles totalling 180°.

One of the limits of geoboards is that they cannot simulate very effectively the transformations that a particular object can undergo if it is pulled or squeezed, for example. Computer programmes can do this but (a cheaper alternative), a 'flickabook' such as you may have used as a child may also be used to good effect. Pimm (1995) suggests that they also make an effective bridge between static images and dynamic sequences. He believes, however, that one of the best ways of creating images can be through words alone,

 *Close your eyes. Imagine a square. Stretch it, shrink it, rotate it, move it around in your mind to get a sense of all the squares it might be.*
(Pimm, 1995, p. 38)

## Concluding remarks

Before I wrote this chapter I considered shape to be a slightly tricky subject to teach: now it seems to be positively fraught with potential difficulties! Having said that I think my investigations have raised some very interesting issues which, I hope, have not only whetted your appetite but also provided you with new and challenging ways to teach shape.

# References

BEN-CHAIM, D., LAPPAN, G. and HOUANG, R.T. (1989) 'Adolescents' ability to communicate spatial information: Analysing and effecting students' performance', *Educational Studies in Mathematics*, **20**, pp.121–46.

CLEMENTS, D.H. and BATTISTA, M.T. (1992) 'Geometry and spatial reasoning', in GROUWS, D.A. (ed.) *Handbook of Research on Mathematics Teaching and Learning*, New York, Macmillan Publishing.

DAVIS, R. (1997) Discussion arising from his paper, 'Postulated cognitive processes in mathematics'. Presented at the 21st conference of the International Group for the Psychology of Mathematics Education.

DESFORGES, C. and COCKBURN, A. (1987) *Understanding the Mathematics Teacher*, London, Falmer Press.

DICKSON, L., BROWN, M. and GIBSON, O. (1984) *Children Learning Mathematics*, London, Cassell.

GAL, H. and VINNER, S. (1997) 'Perpendicular lines — what is the problem? Preservice teachers' lack of knowledge on how to cope with students' difficulties', in PEHKONEN, E. (ed.) *Proceedings of the 21st Conference of the International Group for the Psychology of Mathematics Education (Vol 2)*, Lahti, University of Helsinki.

GRAY, E. (1997) Discussion arising from his paper, 'The nature of the object as an integral component of numerical processes'. Presented at the 21st conference of the International Group for the Psychology of Mathematics Education.

HAYLOCK, D. (1995) *Mathematics Explained for Primary Teachers*, London, Paul Chapman Publishing.

PIMM, D. (1995) *Symbols and Meanings in School Mathematics*, London, Routledge.

TRIADAFILLIDIS, T.A. (1995) 'Circumventing visual limitations in teaching the geometry of shapes', *Educational Studies in Mathematics*, **29**, pp. 225–35.

WILLIAMS, E. and SHUARD, H. (1994) *Primary Mathematics Today* (*4th edn*), Harlow, Longman.

# Chapter 10

# Learning more about children in classrooms

You may well be wondering why on earth I have the audacity to include a chapter on talking to children when a trip into any classroom will instantly demonstrate that 99.9 per cent teachers — even those with little experience — have no difficulty whatsoever in talking to children. In a sense this is certainly true but, if I may be so bold, I would ask you to at least skim through this chapter as you may be surprised by what you find: I was when I heard about some of it.

## Verbalising thoughts

One of the reasons that, comparatively, there has been so little research on young children is that it is sometimes difficult to encourage them to clearly articulate their thinking. Indeed I remember when we were planning the *The Quality of Pupil Learning Experiences* (Bennett et al. 1984) in the early 1980s, a decision was made to focus on 7-year-olds as we might well run into difficulties with younger children being unable to tell us what they were thinking. By this I do not mean that they would have been dumbstruck at the idea of talking to strangers as, indeed, all our researchers were familiar members of the classroom environment. Rather I mean that younger children may have had difficulty putting their thinking into words.

An additional problem may have been that the children would have been less likely than their older colleagues to interpret

FIG 10.1a and 10.1b
Parts 1 and 2 of Piaget's (1952)
Experiment

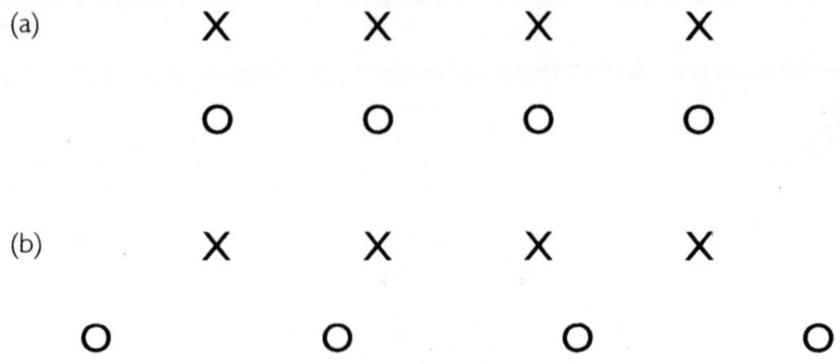

(a)  X    X    X    X

     O    O    O    O

(b)  X    X    X    X

   O       O       O       O

the questions in the way intended. Piaget's work, for example, has been criticised for that very reason. There is no doubt whatever that he added considerably to our insight of young children but it has been suggested that sometimes he made — probably implicit — assumptions about people's interpretation of the tasks set. For example Piaget (1952) reported that children under 7 often had difficulty in conserving numbers. He drew this conclusion from an experiment in which he put out two rows of counters as in Figure 10.1a. If a child agreed that they were the same number of counters in each row, an adult spread out one of the rows (Figure 10.1b) and the child was again asked whether there were the same number of counters in each row. Young children frequently said that there were not.

McGarrigle and Donaldson (1974) questioned the assumptions behind Piaget's thinking arguing that, for a child, an adult's actions often signal a significant change which, together with the repeating of a question, may mean that a different answer is required.

It may be easy to be wise after the event but, as described in Chapter 4, we need to take care when making assumptions about pupil understanding in the light of their responses. Kouba and McDonald (1991) gave a child the following question:

To test this possibility, McGarrigle and Donaldson (1974) used the ingenious idea of a 'Naughty Teddy'. The first part of their experiment was similar to Piaget's — children were presented with two rows of counters as in Figure 10.1a and asked whether there were the same number in each row. A Naughty Teddy then, seemingly accidentally, messed up the counters. When the counters were tidied up, they were as in Figure 10.1b but, unlike Piaget's experiment, there was now a plausible reason for asking the children whether the number of counters was the same in each row. Significantly more children than in Piaget's experiment said that the number of counters in each row was the same.

❛ *Two girls were given three cookies.*
*Three boys were given six cookies.*
*Vicky said, 'That's not fair!'*
*Did Vicky use (or do) math to decide?*      (pp. 107–108)

FIG 10.2
Children's diagram of ping-pong
balls in an egg-box

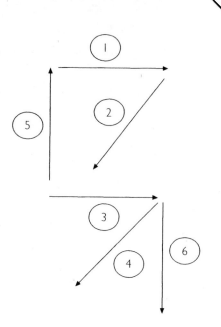

The child's response was that Vicky had not used
mathematics, but it was only when questioned further that
the reasoning behind the answer was revealed, 'she was
too busy talking about boys' (p 108).

Martin Hughes' work (1986) also illustrates that young
children find it easier to demonstrate their knowledge if tasks
are presented within a familiar context: it is relatively easy
to add two and three elephants, for example, but it is quite
another thing to add an abstract pair of numbers such as two
and three.

It is also important to remember that there are other modes
of communication open to you. For example, rather than
asking children to explain something to you, you could ask
them to demonstrate it with objects which come to hand or,
alternatively, they might opt to draw it for you. For example,
on asking two 6-year-olds how many different ways they
could arrange two ping-pong balls in a six space egg-box,
they presented me with Figure 10.2. No words were
required, although I was pleased when, on looking at the
diagram, they appreciated that there was still work to
be done!

As I write this I am reminded of an exercise we were given as undergraduate psychologists: have you ever tried talking while balancing something, such as a pen, on your hand or finger? It is incredibly hard. It may well be therefore that we sometimes make unnecessarily complex demands on some children when we ask them to demonstrate and explain at one and the same time.

## Insight into young children's 'mathematical' thinking

I have written extensively about this elsewhere (1986, 1995) and with Charles Desforges (1987), but here is a potted version for those of you who may be unfamiliar with the idea that some children's aims when doing mathematics may be rather different from our own as teachers.

It would be unwise to generalise, but research suggests that, for some children at least, the aim when doing mathematics is to get the right answer and thus please the teachers. The route to achieving the answer is not important to them and thus, in some cases, you might go so far as to say that whether they use mathematics or not is irrelevant to them as long as the end result is praise and a tick.

Such strategies are not just confined to the less able members of the class although, with more able children, the methods may be faster. For example I watched a 7-year-old memorise the answers to a workcard as the teacher went through it with the class and then scribble the answers down as soon as the demonstration was completed. This observation was confirmed when I asked her afterwards how she had managed to do the work so quickly (Cockburn, 1986).

What I find fascinating is the length some children will go to in order to ensure they obtain the right answer when, in all probability, doing the task mathematically would probably prove quicker and easier. For example, we observed children looking back to earlier pages in their workbook to find the same sum already marked (Desforges and Cockburn, 1987).

FIG 10.3
Gemma's money problem

In another instance I noted Gemma searching through a box of plastic coins in order to see which fitted the shapes in a money problem (see Figure 10.3) (Cockburn, 1986).

A final example which, even after a decade, still raises a chuckle in me comes from Roscoe and Nicola (Desforges and Cockburn, 1987). They had adapted the very convenient strategy of taking it in turns to do the sums they were set. Thus, in effect, they were doing mathematics but at half the rate expected. As it happened their teacher spotted what was going on and the next day, without saying anything, gave them two different worksheets. The children's response to the first four sums are shown in Figure 10.4.

Towards the end of the chapter I will discuss the implications of such observations but, before I do, here is a short task and some more research findings on what goes on in the classrooms.

| **Roscoe's work** | | **Nicola's work** | |
|---|---|---|---|
| T | U | T | U |
| 2 | 8 | 1 | 3 |
| + 3 | 1 | + 4 | 5 |
| 5 | 9 | 5 | 9 |
| | | | |
| T | U | T | U |
| 4 | 0 | 4 | 2 |
| + 3 | 6 | + 3 | 1 |
| 7 | 3 | 7 | 3 |

FIG 10.4
Roscoe and Nicola's work

## Task

When it is convenient take a couple of minutes to ask some children why they think they do sums — or even mathematics — in school. I think you may be surprised by the answers. Over the years I have had a variety of answers to these seemingly straightforward questions: For example some 7-year-olds replied (Cockburn, 1994):

*'Well if you were planning to skid on the grass you might use multilink to make a path.' (Christopher)*

*'Never thought about it.' (Siobhan)*

*'If you are a sailor you might need to add up how far you are from where you need to go.' (Sandra)*

*' 'cos I like doing sums.' (Amy)*

You might also like to ask the children whether they ever see adults doing sums. Again some of the answers I received (Cockburn, 1994) were unexpected:

*'No' (Terri)*

*'No' (Hollie)*

*'No' (Adam)*

*'My uncle 'cos he's a policeman and he had to do maths to get in.' (Jason)*

*'Teachers' (Kim)*

*'My mum: she's a teacher.' (Scott)*

Kouba and McDonald's (1991) works suggests that young children's responses to such questions may not necessarily be taken quite so seriously as one might at first sight. After working with 1,202 pupils in grades K–6 in America they noted that many of the children considered counting to be too easy to be classed as mathematics. Other pupils implied that you could only do one subject at a time — 'you can't read and do math at the same time' (p. 110) — thus artificially restricting the number of occasions such individuals perceived themselves as doing mathematics. Nevertheless children's thoughts on the subject can certainly give pause for reflection and a reassessment of one's actions, as Mrs W discovered when talking to her class of 5-year-olds;

 Mrs W:      Why do you think we need numbers?
Michelle:   So you can spell things.
Mrs W:      Spell things out with numbers?
Antoinette: We need to count the numbers.
Simon:      We need to draw the numbers.
Mrs W:      Why do we need to draw the numbers?
Lisa:       So we can copy them.
Mrs W:      But why do we need numbers at all?
Lisa:       So we can colour them in.   (Cockburn, 1986, pp. 208–9)

## Behind the scenes in mathematics sessions

As I suggested in the case of Nicola and Roscoe, teachers are sometimes aware of some of the subversive activities which go on in the classroom in the name of mathematics. They may also, as in the next example, have an inkling of some of the strategies pupils adopt to avoid drawing attention to themselves,

 . . . they get used to the idea that if I sit here very, very quietly and I don't say anything, she's not going to ask me any question.                    (Mrs. M. in Cockburn, 1986, p. 164)

What I think some teachers may be less aware of is the extent of these activities, both in terms of number and type. For example, having observed well over 100 mathematics tasks in lower primary classrooms, in 24.9 per cent of cases the children did not follow the procedure laid down by their teachers and yet this was not generally apparent when looking at their work (Cockburn, 1986).

To start reflecting on the type of strategies children use, it might be worth casting your mind back to your own school days. Truth be known, when I do that, I come up with very little; this may be down to my great age or the fact I was one of those unimaginative children who enjoyed working her way through pages of sums — certainly the ticks were a source of delight but so too were the calculations.

Tomazos (1997a, 1997b) has come up with some very interesting findings of 11- and 12-year-olds in Australia. The first example illustrates just how difficult it can be for an observant researcher — let alone a busy teacher — to observe just what some children are up to. The account which follows is from the third term of Tomazos' indepth study of a classroom in action. Her work involved detailed observations and discussions with the children (ensuring that both they, and their teacher, were made well aware that confidentiality would be strictly maintained and that no information would be passed between parties). By the time of the extract below, Tomazos felt that the children had relaxed considerably with her and that she was beginning to gain real insight into the classroom processes.

The task the children were set involved investigating whether the different colours of 'smarties' and 'M and Ms' (trade names) were represented in equal proportions in every packet. The first part of the task involved the children working in pairs with two or three tubes of the sweets. They were then asked to go round the class collating the findings of other colleagues. Apparently,

> *A group of girls had initially attempted to collect the data but found they could not keep track of the pairs, and (along with many others in the class) resorted to subversive action. They feigned compliance to the teacher's instruction by overtly 'work-ing' co-operatively and sensibly, but covertly, they falsified their data and exploited the social opportunities made available by the situation.* (Tomazos, 1997a, p. 227)

What is particularly relevant is that *neither* the teacher nor the researcher were aware, at any time that the children were behaving in any way other than that requested by the teacher. Indeed it was not until afterwards, when Tomazos had the following conversation, that the truth was revealed,

> *Karen:    . . . In the end . . . we just wrote down any old thing and just did nothing really, just talked about, like, other stuff and that when she wasn't around.*

*Researcher: Not about the smarties?*

*Sandra:      No, anyway, everyone was doing that, faking it,*
*             not just us.*                         (Tomazos, 1997a, p. 227)

The other example Tomazos gave (1997b) was how children
indicate to the teacher what they think of the work set. An
earlier study by Bennett et al. (1984) had noted that the typical
image of a class of 6 and 7-year-olds was of children,

> *. . . working cheerfully and industriously . . . children always*
> *worked in this way irrespective of appropriateness of the task*
> *set. From the teachers' point of view, children were busy, and*
> *busy work equated with the appropriate demands.*
>
> (Bennett et al., p. 215)

It seems that the older children Tomazos was working with in
Australia, however, had begun to develop ways of indicating
to their teacher what they thought of the work set. They were
aware that they would be in trouble if they were overt in
their messages and so had developed a range of more subtle
strategies. For example, they looked as if they were focusing
on their work but, as the teacher strolled past, they studiously
pretended not to notice him/her and mutter under their breath
something like, 'Oh this is so simple and boring.'

Woods (1990) also describes a range of strategies which
pupils adopt in the classroom. His work tends to be with older
children and does not specifically focus on mathematics but,
nonetheless, it provides some interesting insights into
classroom life.

## Implications

In the light of the above, two important questions spring to mind:
- What implications might such knowledge have on teachers'
  professional practice?
- How do these research findings relate to the basic message of
  this book?

The answers to both questions are closely related in that the aims
of this book and the profession are to help children realise their
mathematical potential. I am not saying that this necessarily means

a raising of standards in the usual sense, for three reasons. The first is that, at time of writing, I think most of us in education are tired of being put down and demoralised by members of local and national government.

Secondly I am yet to be convinced that standards can be raised any further without some reaction elsewhere. For example, if more time is spent on mathematics, it is likely that standards will be raised but where would that time come from? It might mean less time on science, art, history or any of the other primary school subjects and at what cost to children's education in those areas?

And finally, but more positively and fundamentally, I would argue that, if we can increase our own knowledge of mathematics teaching and learning, we can give our children a far better grounding in the subject. If we are to acknowledge and avoid, remove or combat potential problems, it may take longer to educate a child in the meaning of place value but, when we have done it, I would suggest that we have done a far more thorough and worthwhile job than we might previously have done. Having said that, I think we should seriously consider how we can increase our understanding of mathematics education in classrooms, explore whether more pupils can become intrinsically interested in the subject and adopt a more insightful approach to our teaching of mathematics.

# References

BENNETT, N., DESFORGES, C., COCKBURN, A. and WILKINSON, B. (1984) *The Quality of Pupils' Learning Experiences,* London, Lawrence Erlbaum Associates.

COCKBURN, A.D. (1986) *'An empirical study of classroom processes in infant mathematics education,'* Unpublished doctoral thesis, University of East Anglia.

COCKBURN, A.D. (1994) 'Theory and practice: Do student teachers encourage young children's mathematical knowledge in the real world?', in DA PONTE, J. and MATOS, J. (eds.) Proceedings of the 18th Conference of the International Group for the Psychology of Education Volume 4, Lisbon, University of Lisbon.

COCKBURN, A.D. (1995) 'Learning in classrooms', in DESFORGES, C. (ed.) *An Introduction to Teaching*, Oxford, Blackwell.

DESFORGES, C. and COCKBURN, A. (1987) *Understanding the Mathematics Teacher: A Study of Practice in First Schools*, London, Falmer Press.

HUGHES, M. (1986) *Children and Number*, Oxford, Blackwell.

KOUBA, V.L. and McDONALD, J.L. (1991) 'What is mathematics to children?', *Journal of Mathematical Behaviour*, **10**, pp. 105–13.

MCGARRIGLE, S. and DONALDSON, M. (1974) 'Conservation Accidents', *Cognition*, **3**, pp. 341–50.

PIAGET, J. (1952) *The Child's Conception of Number*, London, Routledge and Kegan Paul.

TOMAZOS, D. (1997a) 'Investigating change in a primary mathematics classroom: Valuing the students' perspective', in PEHKONEN, E. (ed.) *Proceedings of the 21st Conference of the International Group for the Psychology of Mathematics Education Volume 4*, Helsinki: University of Helsinki Lahti Research and Training Centre.

TOMAZOS, D. (1997b) Personal communication.

WOODS, P. (1990) *The Happiest Days? How Pupils Cope with School*, London, Falmer Press.

## Chapter 11    Concluding remarks

This book is about broadening our understanding — our understanding of ourselves as teachers and learners; our understanding of mathematics; our understanding of classroom processes; and our understanding of children both as learners of mathematics and as people in a wider world both within and beyond the classroom.

The idea of brainstorming topics is intended as a way of alerting you to potential problems which, in turn, may well point the way to avoiding them or to minimising their potential for damage. It is a technique which can be done relatively quickly to good effect. If you have more time and the inclination, however, you can take longer over the process, discussing it with colleagues, reading, observing pupils and so on.

Whichever strategy you adopt you will be taking a step back from the hurly burly of classroom life. In itself, stepping back will not be new to you for you already do it when planning and reflecting on your classroom practice. It will, though, widen your focus to include more of the complexities of the subject matter you are about to teach. It will also broaden your awareness of the vast amount of knowledge and experience your pupils bring with them as you embark on a 'new' topic. It would be naive to suggest that such insights will immediately transform the mathematics teaching and learning in your classroom. On the contrary, an early reaction may be that, on brainstorming a topic, you may be confronted by so many potential problems that you want to hand in your notice there and then!

It is highly likely that, having read this book, you will begin to notice more and more about individuals and how they are responding to your teaching strategies and the mathematics being presented. This may result in conflicts such as those facing Mrs G in Chapter 9 when she decided not to meet Samantha's specific needs as 'the group might lose interest' (Desforges and Cockburn, 1987, p. 114). That is all too common a dilemma in teaching (Pollard, 1997) and one — with the current class sizes of thirty plus — that is not easily resolved. Indeed it is one of the many challenges of teaching which makes it such a highly skilled profession.

There are three points to bear in mind, however. The first is that changes — perhaps in this case to both your thinking and your practice — are unsettling and tend to skew your attention ( Rudduck, 1991). This will calm down in due course as thinking about potential mathematical problems becomes a more integrated part of your practice.

The second point is that, although all your pupils are unique and each brings different experiences and knowledge to your sessions, general lessons can be learnt from the specific. For example, if you see a child struggling with the addition of tens and units it may be that, although the other children put down the correct answers, there is a general problem. This might be that they have learnt the rules for completing such sums but, as their struggling colleague, they have little or no understanding of the processes involved. Moreover specific problems do not necessarily require individually tailor-made solutions. It may be that you can refer to a scheme or use a game you already have rather than devise a completely new approach for one child. That is not to say that I would wish to discourage you from trying new strategies but rather that one has to be realistic about a teacher's workload.

And, finally, it is my guess that, as you learn more about the knowledge, thoughts and interactions in your classroom, the more you will be interested in teaching and learning and the more likely you are to develop your mathematics teaching with insight. Indeed, as you do so, it is likely that your pupils will begin to establish a more fundamental appreciation of mathematical concepts for, in effect, you will be increasing your ability to relate what you teach to their knowledge and understanding. It is my belief that, by providing your pupils with such a sure mathematical beginning, you will be giving them an excellent and lasting foundation on which to build.

## References

DESFORGES, C. and COCKBURN, A. (1987) *Understanding the Mathematics Teacher*, London, Falmer Press.

POLLARD, A. (1997) *Reflective Teaching in the Primary School*, London, Cassell.

RUDDUCK, J. (1991) *Innovation and Change*, Milton Keynes, Open University Press.

# Index